BEING HERE

A Western journalist's view of Japan

Being Here

A Western journalist's view of Japan

ADRIAN WALLER

A collection of his popular *Japan Times Weekly* columns

YOHAN PUBLICATIONS, INC.

BEING HERE

A Western journalist's view of Japan

A YOHAN LOTUS BOOK /Published 1992

Copyright © 1992 by Adrian Waller

YOHAN PUBLICATIONS, INC.

14-9 3-chome, Shinjuku-ku, Tokyo, Japan

Printed in Japan

For my daughter Nathalie who, in her own way, has shown me how to enjoy Japan.

Books by Adrian Waller

Theatre on a Shoestring

Adrian Waller's Guide to Music

Data for a Candlelit Dinner

The Gamblers

Soulikias: Portrait of an Artist

*Writing! An informal, anecdotal guide to the
  secrets of crafting and selling non-fiction*

*The Canadian Writer's Market,
  Eighth Revised Edition*

*No Ordinary Hotel
  The Ritz-Carlton's first seventy-five years*

Who Stole The Rainbow?

*The Canadian Writer's Market,
  Ninth Revised Edition*

*Being Here
  (A collection of Japan Times Weekly columns)*

CONTENTS

Introduction XI
Acknowledgements XIII
Foreword by Robert J. Collins XV
Kindness beyond words 1
Transported by music 4
Chock-full of socks 7
Really coffee mad! 10
Sanya, the place of no return 14
Ah! This language! 28
Strange paradoxes 31
Japan, anecdotally 34
Teaching the Japanese English 37
Linda's Luck 43
Struggling together 47
Unlearning racism 51
My man Taishi 54
The racist foreigners 57
Tying up loose ends 60
Voices in a house of foreigners 63
Nihonjin classroom 72
My big investment 75
Letter to the PM 78
Business at dinner? 81
Damn, damn lies! 85
The salaried worker's discontent 88
Unseating chauvinism 97
Cup full of luck 100

VIII

Bigotry on Mount Fuji 104
Death of a briefcase 107
Something wrong? 110
Yes, I like Japan 113
Saving souls in Shinjuku 116
Keeping warm 122
Bedeviling English 125
Maybe I'll be back 128
Back in time 131
What a week! 134
The killing of Carmel Ruane 137
Akane's new boots 148
Home, Sweet Home 151
Nihonjin vocabulary 154
Created in Japan 158
Funny goings on 169
Taking back good gifts 172
Comparing life 175
Sexual harassment: The lid is off 178
Up in smoke 184
Heading back 187
Knowing ourselves 190
Have I come full circle? 193
Here, in time 196
Who lost my luggage? 199
Where we live 202
Salt of the earth 205
Hiroshima 208
The ward office 212
'Human fit' jeans 215
Success: a circle 219
I was a 4-1-16-3 222

Like father, like son   226
Hey! They're my shoes!   229
A little bit of love   232
Two up!   236
When mediocrity is beautiful   239
Being myself   243
Unfortunately not made in Japan   246
Let the reporters do their jobs   249
Letter to the folks back home   252

Introduction

I BEGAN WRITING MY little column "Being Here" in *The Japan Times Weekly* in the warm spring of 1990, barely six months after I had arrived in Tokyo from Montreal. It was part of a general renovation plan for the paper as it reached out eagerly for more and more readers.

The actual idea for "Being Here," and what it should try to do, came about in a Tokyo coffee shop one afternoon when my colleague editor Mike Millard and I were working out a course we felt *The Weekly* might follow if it were to be better. We both agreed that if I wrote a weekly piece on page two and our mutual friend David Benjamin did the same on page three, we might help give the paper more personality and warmth. It is to Mike's credit that he took the matter up with our editor, Keisuke Okada, and "Being Here" was born.

It was not, however, always easy to write. Our staff was — and still is — very small, and needed my constant support and guidance. A column, then, had to be written between other work, and lots of it — a weekly deluge of very deep editing, some page layout, and constant teaching.

Because of all this, there were times when column ideas were sparse indeed. It was then that I reminded myself what I had originally set out to do: to write about

Japan as a stranger, and to relate best I could the problems that confront all newcomers when they first arrive here to stay.

Conversely, there were times when, thanks to my wife and friends, ideas never stopped flowing. Then, I was truly in my element as I set out, best I could, to record my life in Japan — as a family man — with a mixture of humor and irony, always honestly and objectively, and most certainly without misgivings.

It goes without saying, I think, that being here in Tokyo has been a lot of fun, and I like to think that some of this shines forth in *Being Here*.

Adrian Waller

Acknowledgements

I am indebted to Keisuke Okada, editor of *The Japan Times Weekly*, and Mike Millard, the general editor, for their encouragement, and to my wife, Irene, for her invaluable help.

My thanks also go to the remainder of the hard-working little *Weekly* staff — Manako Ihaya, Seekay Lan, Yoko Nakamura, Midori Paxton, and Carol Hui — each of whom is reaching for new heights against odds that often seem insurmountable; David Bernat, who proofread my work and made suggestions; David Trokeloshvili, whose help will not be forgotten; Waka Okamura and Takashi Ueno of *The Japan Times'* composing room staff, who helped rescue many of my columns from the belly of the newspaper's big computer.

Finally, how can I possibly forget my readers, without whom my work — and *The Weekly* — would be superfluous?

Foreword

By Robert J. Collins

GENIUS IN ARTISTRY is the unexpected but exquisitely prolonged note in music, the positioning and grace of a brush stroke on canvas, and the delicacy of seasoning and spice in a gourmet dish. It is a special "touch"—an inherent sense of what is right for the creation. In writing, it is the paragraph, the sentence, the phrase, or even just the word that sets the piece artistically. It is neither fancy nor labored. It is merely a string of words put to paper that is, well, just right.

Adrian Waller has that touch. And for all new readers of his work, who join the legions of his current fans, *Being Here* is a book to treasure on several levels.

In the first place, *Being Here* is a series of short articles and observations by a sensitive, observant man who, with his family, makes the cultural leap from the West to Japan with about as much advance preparation as a polar bear might arrange for a spell of larking about in Brazil. Mr. Waller's adventures are *hilarious* (imagine him trying to describe an electric blanket to a shop clerk when his Japanese language skills stretched only to "hello" and "goodbye"), *terrifying* (picture the impact of a call from the visa office at 9 p.m.), *frustrating* (consider the coefficient factor involved in spending half a day opening a bank account), and *touching* (think of the individuals in humanity's mass who go beyond "normal" expectations and do genuinely nice things). All newcomers to Japan have these adventures, but Mr. Waller relates his with that special touch. And his stories become *our* stories.

On a different level, Mr. Waller is a working journalist and columnist. Since 1957, when he began his career as a reporter in England — banging out copy on the city desk, sports desk, the crime watch, reviewing plays and films as a drama critic, and writing entertainment and music reviews — his experience in the print media has been remarkably extensive.

A man who has sold award-winning features articles to scores of magazines, who has authored 11 books, who has written and edited for *Reader's Digest* and *Time*, and who taught writing and journalism at the university level for 20 years, he has seen and commented upon quite a lot. And that perspective, reflected in the pieces in *Being Here* — reprinted from his *Japan Times Weekly* columns — is invaluable to students of modern Japan.

Mr. Waller's observations on the conduct of business, the misconduct of government, and the burrs and prickles in an otherwise homogeneous society, are dead on target. Of particular brilliance is his big piece on the Sanya district of Tokyo — the unmapped flophouse of Japan's hidden drop-outs.

Through it all, however, is the artistry of writing. Mr. Waller arrives in Japan and makes an initial adaptation to it, falls into a groove of comfortable existence, experiences vague discontent and frustration, goes back to his home in Canada, recognizes how he (and his home) have changed, and, without missing a beat in his columns, returns to Japan. The paragraphs, sentences, phrases, and words are there — exquisitely prolonged, graceful, and with just the right seasoning and spice.

Read on. You are in for a treat.

Kindness beyond words

AT A CURBSIDE IN a steady drizzle near Tokyo's busy Shinjuku Station, I learned one of life's great lessons — under a black umbrella. As I waited to cross the street, I suddenly felt the rain stop. A young man had placed his umbrella above my head. Not a word was said, and none was uttered as we walked together for several blocks. Bending to shield me, the man communicated with chuckles of hospitality. I, in return, could only say, "Thank you." I said it a thousand times.

The lesson I learned was that kindness is a language all its own, and one which crosses ethnic boundaries quicker than any other I know except, perhaps, music. You need not speak German to appreciate the mighty symphonies of Beethoven, any more than you need know Japanese to understand — and savor — those moments when Japanese people are opening their hearts.

Once, I spoke to a group of students who aspired to be journalists, seating myself heavily with tiredness before them. In seconds, a man had handed me a cup of hot coffee while another fetched a towel and began to wipe my briefcase and coat. Yes, it was raining in Tokyo — again — which explains why the unsuspecting visitor's first investment is invariably an umbrella.

It also explains why people like me, who are prone

to arthritis, can be virtually crippled by the dampness for days on end.

During one of these episodes, I wanted to buy a walking stick and hobbled from store to store unable to find one. Finally I came upon a little shop in Shinjuku that sold umbrellas and slippers, and went inside. No, said a frail woman, having uncoiled herself from a tatami at the rear of the premises, she did not sell walking sticks. But then, as if suddenly taken over by a divine impulse, her son, who was hovering nearby, said, "Just a minute," and ferreted out an old cane that hung between two cupboards.

It was dusty and worn, and it had been hooked over a bent nail in the shop since the old man who had once leaned so heavily on it had died some five years before. "My Dad was ninety-three when he left us," the shop owner said. Then, handing me the cane with two outstretched arms while his mother looked on, he added, "I know he would like you to have it."

I did not keep that cane, of course. I couldn't. I merely borrowed it until my leg was better, and until I could buy one of my own, then returned it with a little gift of chocolates to acknowledge the kindness. Since then, I have pledged myself to remember all other kind deeds in Japan.

As the weeks rolled on, I began to lose count of all the umbrellas that were placed above my head, and passengers on crowded trains who offered me a seat or relieved me of my packages. Nor could I possibly list all the other occasions when, totally lost, I was at the mercy of an eager Japanese who preferred to take me to my destination rather than try to explain the way to it.

There is also the mundane matter of banking at a Japanese money machine. Thank God for local people who, recognizing a foreigner's dilemma, helped me to draw money when I needed it most. There have been numerous such people as these, including a young woman in Shibuya who insisted on buying me a cup of coffee.

"So you want to practice your English?" I inquired.

"No," came the brisk reply. "I want to know if you've been able to find your way around. Tokyo is a very big city."

It is. God knows it is! So is Yokohama. And it is also big-hearted. When my wife and I asked directions to the city's Chinatown district from a young couple with two children, the man walked back to his house, got his car, picked us up, and took us on a four-hour tour of the area. Again, there were language problems. But again I began to realize just how good intentions, wherever they are rooted, need never be supported by words.

Since being in Japan, I have become aware — and this, I think is far more important than anything — that kindness can be infectious. The other night, in a heavy rain near Shinjuku Station, I met a salaryman who did not have an umbrella, and shared mine with him. I felt it was the proper thing to do.

Again, not a word was said until I muttered, "You'll catch your death of cold."

But the man simply said, "You and I must drink a whiskey together. Oh yes, I would like that! And I pay!"

Transported by music

I NEVER THOUGHT I COULD do it. I never thought for one moment I could ever appear in public with little speakers plugged into my ears, oblivious to the world, shortening the life of my eardrums, and looking moronic in the process. But now I do, shamelessly.

In Tokyo there are things we dislike and, no matter how much we fight, we can do absolutely nothing about them. One is crowds. The other is noise. The two go hand in hand every morning when, against the clanging of a railway station, people literally stuff themselves into commuter trains. As they suffer the crush, men become beasts, women squeaking tyrants. Indeed, Tokyo's rush hour makes us all what we really are not.

I became painfully aware of this just after starting to work for this newspaper. Tired of commuters manhandling me — wrestling me out of carriage doorways, wedging me in places where I preferred not to be, stomping on my feet, wrenching my arms off, knocking my head off, and generally being a nuisance — I decided to do something about it. At first, I grunted and mumbled, and made sure that everyone in the carriage knew what I was feeling. When no one took any notice, I took a different tack.

In Shibuya one morning, a young man charged into the carriage like a Chicago Bears line-backer, ramming me against one of those chrome-plated pipes I had so often felt between my shoulder blades. I decided to fight back by pushing him out. In fact, as the doors closed, the linebacker's arm, hand, and briefcase were inside the train and the rest of him was on the platform, which served him right.

There were also some decidedly uncomfortable journeys. For example, I have made many on only one foot, unable to find enough space for the other. Worse, there were times when I was forced to be close — very close — to someone I didn't much care for. My friends always seem to get fresh-scrubbed women. I, on the other hand, am invariably pinned against old drunks, or other people with strong breath. Suffice it to say, that if I am to cuddle someone, I'd like to choose who that someone is going to be.

All this brings me to the earphones. A colleague editor, bless him, gave me the best bit of advice I've received in Japan. The only way to beat Tokyo's rush hour, he said, was not to try to beat it, but to join it. And there were things I could do to actually make my 90-minute trip to work pleasant each day. One, I could try finding carriages that contained an abundance of perfumed women. Two, I could use a walking stick in the hope that fellow commuters might take compassion on me and give me a seat. Thirdly, I might make myself oblivious to the mess if I zoomed around the Yamanote Line listening to my favorite composers.

Every morning since, I have done what I've so often told my young daughter not to do. I have isolated myself from the world. But I have done so to enjoy some of the best music ever composed. Now, I can report that Beethoven's *Rhapsody for Piano, Chorus, and Orchestra,* or any one of Mozart's exquisite 27 piano concertos, bestows a majesty even on such desolate places as Takadanobaba Station. Try this yourself, and you'll discover, as I have, that tired, leaden feet can shuffle up and down grimy steps in time to melody.

The other night, however, there were serious repercussions. While engrossed in Mahler's towering *Symphony No.2,* I entered the wrong train. An express, it took me 12 stations too far before I realized what had happened. On the return trip, more transported by this noble music than ever, I missed my stop again and ended up where I had originally started out.

I finally reached my destination just as the symphony thundered to its close. It was as if Gustav Mahler had tailored it especially for the occasion.

"Taking the wrong train," a friend later observed, enabled you to hear something good in its entirety. Perhaps you should do it more often."

I have promised myself I will. Through music I will learn to enjoy the entire Tokyo rail system.

Chock-full of socks

I MAKE NO EXCUSES FOR IT. I love socks. Whenever I am let loose in a store, the sock counter is the first thing I look for. Once, I almost missed a flight because I became preoccupied with comparing socks in a duty free shop. In Hollywood, Fla., my favorite hangout was the Sock Exchange, which sold designer hosiery. Unfortunately, it closed for the want of more people like me to keep it going.

For the most part, I like long socks that stop just below the knee, and preferably ones with a quiet pattern. In my search for perfect socks, however, I will look at any — long ones, short ones, and those that are red, yellow, mauve, even white.

The older I have become, the more socks have consumed me. Maybe I am derived from cracked genes or disfigured chromosomes. Sigmund Freud would doubtless have diagnosed other causes, though: that at the age of seven, I was probably in love with a rhinoceros. Or he might have simply left me alone. Some people collect postcards, birds' eggs, even license plates. I collect socks, and revel in it.

The first thing I noticed about Tokyo was that it is a sock collector's paradise. Socks are everywhere. They hang in tobacco kiosks, supermarkets, even liquor stores. In Ueno, they dangle above a fish counter. And while I enjoy possessing socks, the Japanese like selling them to me — three pairs for ¥1,000, sometimes four. In this way, Japan and I are made for each other.

A few weeks ago, a friend phoned urgently to say he'd seen *five* pairs of socks for ¥1,000 and thought I should hurry out to buy them before they all sold. I did, even though it was raining. Socks, after all, are about the only things cheaper in Japan than in North America. And for this, a lot of us can be truly grateful.

I don't need a Sigmund Freud to tell me why I'm sock mad. Nor do I need Japan's trade minister to explain why his country sells so many of them to me. The answers, I think, are obvious. I have amassed some 50 or 60 pairs of socks over the months because, as a child growing up in war-torn England, I only ever had two pairs — one on my feet, the other waiting for my mother to find the time to wash it. I wore the same socks for several years, it seemed, long after I had grown out ot them, and long after there was not very much of them left for my mother to darn.

They were never nice socks either, and they rarely ever stayed up long enough to make my legs itch. They formed instead a concertina around the tops of my boots. Thus, the family album bears witness to the truth: Socks and I were not compatible at all. But I told myself that some day I would own some proper socks that looked as if they had been lacquered onto my calves — just like the ones in Japan.

Over the years, I have come to view socks as a symbol of affluence, particularly knitted ones that are exquisitely plaided. Also over the years, Japan has consumed socks like throwaway chopsticks. Stockinged feet are a Japanese way of life, as is walking long distances from home to train, and from train to office. Socks are more visible here. Next time you are seated on a train, please note this for yourself.

When you see that very short socks reveal little expanses of white-waxed leg, you will understand why I prefer long socks, and that nothing looks quite as ridiculous as white ones with a dark suit, or any other shade of suit come to that. Years ago, when purely for financial reasons a visit to Japan was out of the question for me, I encountered an aged editor who convinced me that a man's character was immediately established by the state of his shoes and the length and color of his socks. I have never forgotten this. Nor has my wife. That is why, when Christmas rolls around, or Easter, Valentine's Day, my birthday, or any other such kind of day, she pokes a little bag at me as though it were hot. It usually contains . . . guess what? You have it. Socks.

Regretfully, these gifts are decreasing with disturbing regularity. Now we live in Japan, my wife says I can buy my own bloody socks. I will. And if she isn't careful, I'll select brilliant red ones, or even those of a fluorescent pea green — socks that will make my old editor shudder in his grave.

Really coffee mad!

MY CLOSEST FRIEND IN JAPAN these days happens to be a colleague at *The Japan Times*. He's a large, gregarious, lumbering American with a voice of thunder and a laugh of great chimes. To see Big Mike and me together — he with his rucksack and black leather jacket, and me toddling beside him in my English tweed coat, and carrying a briefcase — you'd probably wonder what on earth we had in common. In many ways, however, we are surprisingly compatible, and with healthy, eclectic tastes.

We both like sports, music, politics, food, women, and a couple of other things that cannot be mentioned here. We also agree, I think, that we enjoy being in Japan and that if we were wealthy here, and no longer needed to work, we would be more than happy to spend our entire days sitting in coffee houses reading poetry and great novels.

Sometimes, though, I would like to wring Big Mike's bloody neck, and the only thing that stops me is that it's as thick as an oak tree. Indeed, this man, who once tried his hand as a heavyweight boxer, felling people much larger than himself with a single blow to the shoulder, is built very much like a cement mixer.

Not long ago, and feeling spring welling up in his expansive Oregon heart, Mike suggested that we go to Shinjuku to browse in a book store. On the way, he made it known in his big voice that he wanted his mid-afternoon coffee first. So the moment we got off the train, he led me toward a coffee shop he knew near Shinjuku Station. "It's pretty half-decent," he promised. "Lots of atmosphere. Lots of character. You'll like it."

"You sure?" I inquired.

"Of course I'm sure," Big Mike responded, a little hurt that I should question his judgment. "Anyways, have I ever lied to you?"

He hadn't, of course. But when we got to this — one of his favorite places — the customers, most of them salarymen who should have been working, were either reading the newspaper or sleeping. The thing that irked me most about it, though, was the bill: Two coffees cost ¥1,600. Since Mike and I always go dutch when we eat out together (except on those occasions when I am without money), I actually ended up paying ¥800 for a single cup of coffee. True, it came on a silver tray with a little jug of cream and a bowl of sugar, but, for that price, it should have been served with brandy in a gold chalice.

Mike doesn't know this — and won't until he reads what I have to say about it — but I've not been able to rid this ¥800 from my mind. It's not that I can't afford it. I can. It's purely a feeling I have — that no cup of coffee can ever be worth ¥800, not in Shinjuku, not in Buckingham Palace. My frustration also has to do with being sucked in.

On my way home, I began surmising what I could have done with this money elsewhere. I mean, for $7 U.S. in a little bar I know in Manhattan, we could both get half-plastered. Had we wanted to get completely plastered, we could have bought a bottle of bourbon and drunk it in a parking lot.

Talking of drinking, I don't much like it because I can't afford it. But I sure know why the Japanese do. As a friend in the newsroom says, "When you suffer through the bigotry, the racism, the price of things — and this godawful notion the Japanese have that they're somehow a bunch of elitists — it's enough to drive anyone to drink." And coffee houses are institutions in Japan because a lot of Japanese feel the urge to escape from it all.

Yet a coffee is often more expensive than a beer.

But getting back to Big Mike. Newspaper people are quite often known to develop addictions to smoking, drinking, and coffee, and I've know some who were addicted to other things, too. My friend Mike, though, doesn't smoke, and never has, drinks only socially, but has a consuming passion for strong coffee. Every workday morning, he lumbers into the elevator with not just one take-out coffee, but two. And, were I not with him during some lunch hours, he would spend more money on coffee than he would on meat and vegetables.

The most disconcerting thing, though, is that he thinks absolutely nothing of it. Yet, what he so often buys — as was the case in Shinjuku — is not merely a cup of coffee, but only *half* a cup of coffee. That makes me madder than I was when I first began writing this. It's as bad as paying ¥200 yen for half a loaf of bread, or ¥300 for a glass of milk with so many large clumps of ice in it, that there's comparatively little milk in the glass. Someone is making a lot of money out of gullible Tokyoites, but that's not Big Mike's fault. Or is it? The reason I want to wring his neck is that he's made me a part of it. And, since I take neither cream nor sugar in my coffee, I should be paying less for it.

Sanya, the place of no return

IT'S ELEVEN O'CLOCK ON A steamy May morning and Nurse Rita Burdzy, a Maryknoll sister, is on her daily rounds of her patients — talking to them, listening to them, holding their hands. They do not rest in hospital beds, though, for these patients are men like S-san, who lies motionless on the first bench on the left as you enter the local park, or H-san, who has spent every night for the past seven months in a shop doorway where the Hibiya Line thunders high above the main street, and where he has long since become impervious to the noise.

Or they are such men as N-san, who fell drunk one night with part of one leg resting on the railway line. Now minus his left foot, he lives in an alleyway not far from another of Sister Rita's patients — a man whose hands were amputated after he had burned them in the bonfire he'd built a couple of Christmases ago, to keep warm.

In modern-day Japan such poverty is not only disquieting, but a strange phenomenon, indeed, and there is a striking parallel to it virtually on its doorstep. Every workday night, the trains that draw into Minami-senju Station discharge thousands of white-shirted salarymen who flock, like locusts, to homes in adjoining districts to eat a hot dinner with their families. Yet, in bleak, foreboding Sanya, a featureless flatland of derelict bars and grubby noodle shops that is bordered by the crook of the Sumida River in Tokyo's north-east corner — a mere one square-kilometer of gray streets, grime, and pollution — about 15.5 percent of the area's entire population of 45,000 people are single men who have nowhere else to sleep but on a communal tatami in one of the nearly 200 "flop houses" that cost ¥800 a night.

Most of these men went to the neighborhood to look for part-time work, for which they are paid daily — packing, perhaps, loading many of the trucks that thunder nearby, or working in construction. But life was not good to them all. What concerns Sister Rita most of all are the 1,200 men who do not, or cannot, find work and must bed down in public places. Most are without food or money. Many can barely muster the strength to stand up.

The very same men who must sleep on Sanya's streets tonight, they lack ambition, hope, or love — save for that offered in the parks, alleyways, and gutters by Sister Rita, a former U.S. army nurse, and a colleague Maryknoll missionary named Sister Elizabeth Kato, a chubby, optimistic Hawaiian Japanese who started her career as a teacher. Together, the two women run a drop-in center known as the Sanyu-kai. Roughly translated, the Japanese characters used to write it mean mountain, friend, and group.

"So," says Sister Rita, "we consider ourselves friends of the poor people of Sanya as they start the long climb back." Adds Sister Elizabeth, "We are two people in a group of volunteers who, in our own small way, are trying to upgrade the quality of life of street people. It is an uphill battle."

It is. The center, which meets Sanya's growing problem head-on and pragmatically, stands where it somehow belongs — in a narrow Sanya street whose only distinguishing mark is a long, blank wall. Appropriately, it is flanked by a dismal drinking establishment and a karaoke bar.

At its heart, and the reason for its being, is a clinic that is staffed by Sister Rita and any one of seven volunteer doctors who sees about 30 patients a day. Since the center opened five years ago, in fact, approximately 1,800 different men, more than half of them over 50, have sought treatment in its clinic a total of nearly 15,500 times. Of these, 80 percent have been raging alcoholics suffering severely from all manner of alcohol-related problems: cirrhosis of the liver, urinary infections, internal bleeding, ulcers, and depression. Some have sat at a curbside for many hours hallucinating; a dozen or so are still "seeing" visions and "hearing" noises when the clinic's physician-on-duty examines them.

"When did you start drinking recently?" the doctor asks.

He seeks to differentiate between hallucinations caused by such deep-rooted psychiatric problems as schizophrenia or manic depression that may have been caused by loneliness or trauma, or those brought on by excessive liquor.

Additionally, nearly all the men have been afflicted by one, or a combination of, other ailments: malnutrition, hypertension, diabetes, tuberculosis, fatigue, or general inertia.

"What's the use in carrying on when you can see no

way out?" says a former farmer from Hokkaido, who has been living on Sanya's street for four years. Adds another, a one-time stableman from Osaka, "The real trouble with this life is that you settle down for the night with a buddy right next to you to keep you warm, but you never know if, in the morning, you're gonna find each other dead."

Behind the fatalistic humor lies the dreadful truth. Last year alone, more than 150 of those men who had made the streets of Sanya their permanent homes died there — nearly all of them where they slept. They either froze to death during winter or had sought help for their sicknesses far too late. Several were struck by cars when they wandered aimlessly from the sidewalks, or by trains when they staggered near the railway tracks. A few were attacked by a gang of thugs and had oozing knife wounds to prove it. At least three are thought to have been murdered.

A study, by Tadako Miyashita of the North Tokyo Welfare Center, found that residents of Sanya — in a country which boasts that its people can expect to live longer that those of any other — were dying at the rate of one every 2.69 days, and at an average age of 54, mostly from over drinking. "So statistically," says Sister Rita, "if more don't die in the summer from medical problems made considerably worse by dehydration from the heat, they will do so in the winter from the cold. That is a fact."

A blond, raw-boned woman of 38 with compassionate eyes and a long, loping stride, Sister Rita is so fluent in both written and spoken Japanese that she was able to rewrite her entire nursing examinations, just so she would be able to practice her profession in Sanya. "But," she says wistfully, "a lot of needs are not really being met here."

For those without the stamina to walk, the clinic is an eternity away; other men are far too proud to concede that street life has conquered them. And, while dozens have existed in Sanya for a matter of weeks, literally hundreds have done so since before Sister Rita left her native Missouri to become a Maryknoll missionary 12 years ago.

The three-story center she helps run, with its short flight of steps striking steeply from the dusty street, was tailor-made for a place like Sanya. During Japan's long period of Shogun rule — the Edo period, between the 13th and 19th centuries — the district was, as the *Far Eastern Economic Review* once put it, "a repository for the bottom of Japanese society." It has since been so shunned by Tokyo's middle classes as a place to stay away from that it does not appear on any city map. For all this, Sanya's history cannot be ignored. It was there, after all, in one of old Tokyo's main execution grounds, that 200,000 people were supposedly beheaded, crucified, or slashed to death, for their crimes.

In Japan's rush into modernization, during the Meiji period, which dawned in 1868, the remains of these "criminals" began to be found when municipal workers turned the soil to build the main road that leads from Minami-senju Station. This is now called "The Road of Bones," and the thoroughfare that crosses it is known as Namidabashi, the "Bridge of Tears." This is because it was once a small river that separated the realm of criminals and outcasts from the city that had expelled them. Here, on a small bridge, Edo-era families said goodbye to errant relatives as they were dragged to the other side of the river — and the other world.

From these early times, superstitious Tokyo has not only looked upon Sanya as the province of its lower classes, but as a place from which there could never be any return. End up in Sanya, they still say, and you will never leave. Few people ever do.

Since World War II, relatively cheap land prices have beckoned dozens of small businesses, and Sanya has emerged as, perhaps, the country's day-labor capital. When Tokyo prepared for the 1964 Olympic Games, an estimated 15,000 men lived there — primarily while building roads — in 400 flop houses. Many never left because they revelled in both the big city and the average ¥7,000 they were paid, regularly, almost every day. If they weren't already doing so, they began to drink heavily and gamble. Those who had nowhere else to go hung around hoping for better times that never came.

Thus a center like this was needed. And it wasn't too long in coming. It's beginnings can be attributed to three men — Father Bill Grimm, a Maryknoll priest, a Japanese psychiatrist named Masahiko Katori who had been working at a Sanya welfare center for more than 20 years, and Father John Meeney, himself a recovering alcoholic who had brought Alcoholics Anonymous to Japan, forming an organization called the Maryknoll Alcohol Center in nearby Minowa. Grimm, a big, gray-bearded New Yorker was working as a fund raiser for MAC, as the organization later got to be called, and felt that the only way to reach out to the alcoholics of Sanya was by opening a center there.

Shrewdly, however, Meeney conceded that the AA program would not necessarily be effective for all the men he wanted to help. "And these must not be ignored," he said. Remembers Sister Rita, "He wanted to provide a place where the homeless would be treated humanely — where they would feel safe, welcome, loved, and listened to." Meanwhile, both Grimm and Katori recognized that Sanya's population was aging, and that so many street people were lonely, hungry, and in need of the kind of medical attention they could not get in government-sponsored clinics. If patients had alcohol in their systems, these organizations immediately turned them away.

"So a center that provided both a meeting place and a clinic was born," Sister Elizabeth, 51, recalls. And it finally opened its doors in rented, storefront premises on October 17, 1984, just in time for a long, hard winter. In 1989, thanks to good donations, it bought a plot of land and erected a building of its very own, which is manned today by nearly 50 volunteers — a group of people who are united by their desire to serve those who have been left out of Japan's economic miracle. They range from a freelance photographer and a middle-aged Japanese man who counsels the terminally ill, to a 16-year-old high school student and a mother of three children, the wife of a credit company president.

The volunteers also include Sister Rita and Sister Elizabeth, whose work seems endless. Several of those flop houses, which at least kept men warm and out of the gutters, have closed. More homeless men still keep arriving, and soulless Sanya is not only a mess, but a blot on Japanese society. While local municipal officials claim there are enough jobs to go round, a lot of the homeless are too drunk or too sick to work, anyway. Others hold down a job for as many days as it takes them to stock up on cheap liquor and food, then they hit the streets again with everything they own either stuffed into their pockets, or packed neatly in a plastic bag they have found in a garbage bin.

Understandably, they cannot resist a place to talk. For those who are still sufficiently sober, it is the highlight of their day to sit in the little lounge and chat to another volunteer, a 45-year-old Roman Catholic deacon from Quebec, Canada, named Jean LeBeau. Throughout most of their long day, in fact, about 100 of the men stop by for a cup of green tea with him. When it is raining or unusually hot, some 30 or so line their shoes neatly on the steps and sit cross-legged around the three folding tables there, swapping stories. They know they have struck absolute rock bottom, and the center is their only link with the *other* world, the one they would like to be a part of.

The men seek solace in that little lounge. Alcohol and sickness has severed their marriages, estranged them from their families, and isolated them among friends — even those they once knew on the street. A lot are depressed by not having found work on that day, or on any recent one, come to that. They want to talk about their lives, their fears, their hopes, their sicknesses, and their injuries. "Or they just want to be with someone," LeBeau says. "Their greatest misery is loneliness."

One man, however, arrived at the center to share

good news that had filtered through to him — that his 26-year-old daughter had married. Only too well did he know why he had not been invited to the wedding.

The centre's second floor is a daycare center for people over 60, run by Sister Elizabeth. It's third floor consists of a small tatami room for a live-in volunteer and an office where donations of food, clothing, and money are recorded. It costs ¥10 million a year to run the Sanyu-kai, and it is money well spent

As she covers her rounds, her long stride shortening, Sister Rita spots a large, blue plastic tarpaulin stretched between two trees and an iron railing in the corner of Tamahime Park. She gives it only a passing glance and shrugs with hopelessness, having seen this make-shift home many times before, though not always in the same spot. When city workers arrive to clean Sanya's streets they tell whoever happens to be living there — summer or winter — to move on. Invariably, the occupants oblige. Before departing, however, they call in at the center. "Don't worry about us," they tell the volunteers. "We'll be gone for a few days. But if you want to talk to us, we'll be back," Within a week or so, they are.

"Hey, Sister!" one of them cries out on that steamy May morning. "Come and look at my leg!"

Sister Rita does. The limb has been so badly burned that it is weeping profusely under the haphazard bandaging.

"You'd better come and see us this afternoon," Sister Rita tells the man. "I think the doctor should see that wound. It maybe turning septic."

Two other men under that make-shift roof are

oblivious to the world, the noise, and the pollution. So is a middle-aged woman. The only splash of optimism is yet another man — another Sanya fixture — who lives against a fence next to a noodle joint just across the road. A wiry, gregarious little man with twinkling eyes, Toshi, as he is known, tells passersby that when ABC News visited Tokyo from America a couple of years before, a producer asked him to play his harmonica. Performing on the street for a vast American audience remains Toshi's only claim to fame. The rest of his life is in tatters, and probably always will be.

Not far away, in an alleyway behind a moss-covered shrine, Sister Rita spots Y-san, the man without hands. He is slumped, as he always is, against a wall. Because of heavy drinking the night he lit his bonfire, he lost what a nurse like Sister Rita calls "peripheral sensation in his extremities," most notably his arms and legs. Neither did he know, in his drunken stupor, just how close to the flames he really was.

Proud and independent, Y-san was in hospital several times for treatment to his stubs, but, on each occasion he missed the freedom of the street, and discharged himself. He has no money but, like most of the other vagrants who pass through Sanya, does not beg. "Beyond soliciting the odd cigarette," says Sister Elizabeth, "most of the men here ask for nothing. They would rather eat only what they can find for themselves."

Indeed, to be successful as a hobo entails keeping a careful record of which restaurants serve what food, and making sure that you are in the vicinity when the left-overs are being tossed away. Thus, on most evenings, the fitter men of Sanya, and those who have enough cash for the subway fare down to Ginza or Roppongi, stake out those garbage cans that, traditionally, yield the finest cuisine. Then they retreat into the shadows of Sanya to eat it.

The men also know that organizations like the Sanyu-kai, and others that have risen up in Sanya in recent years to meet their needs, freely distribute whatever food they have. Three times a week, Sister Elizabeth serves the homeless hot, chicken broth and rice, which she cooks herself. Whoever else happens to be on duty distributes cookies that are sent regularly from a Trappist monastery in Hokkaido. And when winter closes in, volunteers combine with the Sisters of Charity, just along the road, to run a twice-weekly soup kitchen. The line-up has been known to stretch for four, long blocks.

Different faces, haggard, worn, and vacant are seen on Sanya's streets all the time. More will continue to be so. Many of the flop houses are slowly being replaced by business hotels that are charging as much as ¥2,500 a night, and which more men will not be able to afford. Apart from those who have made the district their home, others have been drifting through it for 20 years from other day-labor centers — Kamagasaki in Osaka, Sasajima in Nagoya, and Kotobukicho in Yokohama. "There seem to be occasions," says Sister Rita, "when someone we haven't seen for ages just suddenly reappears. One day, out of thirty patients, we will have five new ones. At other times, we will see only those people we've known for five years."

But whoever they are, and however unclean they may be, Sister Rita finds kind words for them all, marveling at how they observe the unwritten rules of street life, how they have created a sub-culture, a sort of sub-society that knows few boundaries. For the most part, the men don't cheat each other, don't lie, and don't encroach on each other's territory without first being invited. "In general," says Sister Rita, "they are wonderful guys who came to Sanya in an honest way looking for honest work but who, because of circumstances that were sometimes beyond their control, were unable to work for a long period of time."

But what about those who are already drunk when, clad in blue jeans and a floral blouse or T-shirt, she embarks on her mid-morning rounds? "It's amazing," Sister Rita says. "We see men who are so drunk they can barely rise from the sidewalk. But then, the following day, we'll see them coming home from a job. They're not lazy — they showed a willingness to work — just sick."

A few year back, when her father died, she returned to the United States for two months and was sorely missed. On the day she returned to Sanya, a group of men huddled outside a liquor store in the rain poured across the road to greet her. "Rita," one man said. "We prayed for you, and we prayed for your dad and your family." And when the center moved to its present building a year or so ago, about two dozen patients turned out to help carry files, furniture, and medical equipment.

Sanya's successes have been both meager and modest, and the Maryknoll sisters know it only too well. A handful of men have actually sobered up, found steady work, and left Sanya to rent an apartment. One is a former fishmonger of 57, who tried to burn out the tattoo on his right arm with acid and spent nights in so much pain that he walked and walked until he could stand it no more. Seen by the clinic doctor, he was immediately referred to a hospital where the limb was amputated. Perversely, the only reason he could afford to pay rent was because he began to receive a government disability pension.

The greatest success of all was probably the 44-year-old former warehouseman. Alcohol — and the acute depressions and hallucinations it brought with it — had driven him into an institution for the mentally ill more than 20 times. Recently, however, he was admitted to hospital with pains, and, the day before he was due to be discharged, suffered a grand mal seizure that sent him into a deep coma. The last thing Sister Rita heard about him was that a group of his Alcoholics Anonymous friends were arranging his funeral.

Miraculously, after two days the man recovered and was discharged. He headed straight for the center where he broke down and wept.

"I realize now that I must really re-evaluate my life," he said. "I must find out why I've been spared after suffering that coma. I mean, I should be dead."

All this was six years ago. Since then, the man has found both a job and a room — and has not had a single swig of alcohol. Says Sister Rita, "When a person truly realises just where he had gone wrong, he is well on the way to a wonderful recovery." Another patient, however, who also stopped drinking for six years and who took a social welfare course to equip him to help his former street buddies, was last seen back where he was before — on the *second* bench as you enter Tamahime Park, not far from the man without hands, the man who lost his foot, and the blue tarpaulin.

While heading back to the Sanyu-kai to open that afternoon's clinic, Sister Rita remembers him. A tear or two fills her eyes, and her soft voice trembles. "Maybe," she says, "just maybe, if we all looked at a homeless man and said to ourselves that this could be our father, our brother, or our uncle. . . well maybe it would help us all understand."

Ah! This language!

A FEW WEEKS AGO I BEGAN a long hunt for a printer for my IBM-compatible computer. But, wherever I went, I was greeted with the same two simple words: "No stock." Did this mean the shop in question actually sold printers like the one I wanted but was waiting for a new shipment? Or did it mean that it had no intentions of ever doing so? Unless I retrace my steps with an interpreter, I'll never know. More certain is that trying to make myself understood here has consumed an inordinate amount of my energy, and not always with positive results.

Opening a bank account was one problem, about which I will tell you another time. So was trying to retrace a parcel I left on the Chuo Line. How could I explain that it contained both a book and a chicken pie? I gave up the business of trying to find it in utter despair.

Once, I bought what I thought was shampoo and wondered why it never lathered. It turned out that I had acquired another bottle of hair conditioner instead. Conversely, a friend once bought what he thought was a special cream for delicate skin and became suspicious of his purchase when, that very day, he ventured out in the rain. His arms were suddenly amass with little bubbles. He had bought liquid soap.

Another friend who was unable to either speak or read Japanese bought cheese and some potatoes, slicing them carefully and putting them into a microwave oven with some cooking oil. The combination, he thought, might make a fine meal. When the time came for him to serve it, however, his guests suffered in silence. He had cooked the potatoes in lemon-scented dish washing liquid.

A foreign teacher, meanwhile, tells how his mother, overwhelmed by the selection at the Isetan perfume counter, couldn't resist applying herself liberally with free samples. All eyes fell upon her as she cocked her head to one side and sprayed her neck with shaving foam. The staff, I'm told, could barely contain their laughter.

A few days later — and this example could have had serious repercussions — that same woman sprinkled what she thought was spice onto a pizza, but which happened to be a rodent killer. Fortunately, neither she nor her husband fell ill.

The greatest problem I had, reared itself uncompromisingly when I decided to buy an electric blanket. Out came my pencil and a piece of paper on which I drew an oblong, holding it up for all to see. The clerk shook his head, then scurried off and returned with a woman. Both perused the oblong with interest, discussing it to some length. Then the woman showed me a table cloth. Could it be that?

"No," I said, "it couldn't. You cannot sleep on a table cloth."

Into the oblong I then drew the figure of a prostrate man with a smile of satisfaction upon his bearded face. This time, the two employees tilted their heads, tutted, hummed, scratched their temples, admired my drawing

— and took on very grave looks. Then they beckoned me to the carpet department.

"No," I said. "But you're getting closer."

It was Saturday afternoon, and I couldn't have picked a worse time for this. Japanese people must know what electric blankets are. It gets cold enough for them.

I strung together what I thought was perfect Japanese — sort of pidgin Japanese, if you like: *"Electrico blanketo."* It served only to confuse even more. The employees scratched their tilted heads again, and hummed a little more.

Finally, there was nothing else for it. I had to do it. I put down my bags, took off my shoes, rolled out a small carpet, and lay on it in a fetal position pretending to be asleep. Bingo! I was relieved to see a sense of realization creep across the faces of all who had gathered to watch me.

That's how I eventually bought what I wanted. The two other electric blankets I returned for later, for my wife and daughter, were acquired with relative ease because I had not been forgotten, and probably never will be. The store's entire third-floor sales staff — at Peacock, in Iogi — haven't often encountered a foreigner playing charades on a Saturday afternoon before.

I found a printer, by the way. At first, a receptionist stiffened and, without even looking at me, said, "No stock." But after I'd spoken to her boss, an American, one was discovered immediately. Next week, if I can muster the energy, I will start Japanese lessons.

Strange paradoxes

BY THE RECKONING OF ALL who saw me eating a bar of chocolate at Tamachi Station at the height of rush hour the other day — and who, like most Japanese, believe that eating in public is impolite — I have been a very naughty boy. I admit that. The first thing I do on leaving the train each morning is buy myself a Snicker's to eat on my way to my office. Quite simply, I need chocolate to start my day, even if it *does* mean devouring it in the street.

If I could speak Japanese and had a public address system, I would ask all of Tamachi if it would prefer me to eat chocolate in public, or do some of the other things there that Japan accepts — like urinating, vomiting from drunkenness, and, of course, spitting. Indeed, the entire episode raises some of the baffling contradictions that make this country both fascinating and difficult.

It is culturally wrong, for example, for women to show bare legs, even at the height of a hot summer. They must always wear hose. Mixed toilets in the workplace are common, however, and mixed sulfuric baths — the *onsen* — are not unusual. Since the Japanese confess to being inordinately modest, all this seems strange indeed.

More so is that vast numbers of men read sex-oriented comic books, most of them, by the standards of progressive Western societies, downright illegal because they show sexual violence at its very worst — businessmen disrobing school girls, and women in various stages of submission. If this juvenile junk satisfies sexual fantasies, so be it. But why does the law permit it on trains — for school girls to see?

In Japan, it's illegal to smoke before the age of 20, yet teenagers are the heaviest smokers of all, and tobacco companies hire pretty women to hand them cigarettes as promotional ploys. No one is ever arrested for it.

To reduce promiscuity, the Japanese Government has declared birth control illegal. Abortions, however, are not only legal but a huge business. And condoms, half-dozen packets costing an even ¥1,000 — and no tax, by the way, to spare a man the indignity of having to wait for change — are freely available.

Despite the government's disturbing inconsistency, this land of institutionalized love hotels is much more promiscuous than anyone will admit. Yet, virginity is so sacred that "fallen" women find it difficult to meet life-long partners. Quite often, divorced women are ostracized by their families, and they must live in public dormitories until they can rake up enough money for a deposit on an apartment — if, that is, they can search out a landlord who is broad-minded enough to rent them one. Many landlords will not rent to unmarried couples who want to live together.

Yes, the Japanese are quiet, reserved people. So much so that they will not speak until they are spoken to, will not venture opinions, and will not confront either a friend, a co-worker, or the system — however strong their grudges may be. They are quite happy, however, to fight for a seat on a train. Kimono-clad women, many of them quite aged, are seen prodding and pushing their way into a packed carriage. It is culturally all right to do so.

But that is not all. As soon as their children are born, Japanese mothers register them into a kindergarten — and, over recent years, into pre-kindergartens — to better equip them to attend a cram school later, and, eventually, a fine university. Because rich people are privileged in these matters, no matter how bright their children may be, mothers buy themselves Gucci shoes and expensive coats to give school officials "the right impression." Finally in university, however, their sons and daughters do little useful work, and virtually no research. They simply wait to be offered a job — for life.

Japan is rich. It's a miracle, but it's true. Nonetheless, its living conditions are pitiful. People exist in rabbit-hutch housing, almost all of it unheated at the height of cold, damp winters, and workers make very low salaries with which they must pay the world's highest prices for almost everything.

The uncomplaining Japanese are even content to make less money than their Japan-based Western counterparts because Westerners are revered and too many Japanese consider themselves inadequate by comparison. Against the rest of Asia, however, they see theirs as "a pure race." Thus, as we've heard from the Chinese, the Koreans, and the Filipinos, bigotry is rife and life in Japan could be better for them.

So long as I'm here, I'll continue to enjoy my morning Snicker's.

Japan, anecdotally

A READER HAS ASKED ME to recall those anecdotes that most vividly depict my view of Japan. There was one proviso, however. All had to be rooted at *The Japan Times*. I could, of course talk about the inevitable struggle in bringing out a newspaper, and the time an ingenious but silly staffer poked around inside a colleague's computerized story file and meddled with his words, but I won't. True to the request, I relate those little anecdotes that show what life here is really all about.

A senior colleague tells how, when working the late shift, he'd arrive home at 1 a.m., sleep until 9 a.m., enjoy his first cup of coffee in his little garden, then spend an hour or so — still clad in his yukata — tending his plants. One day, his wife got a surprise call from the local welfare officer assigned to keep vigil over the neighborhood.

"Does your poor husband need help?" he asked.

"No, why?" was the surprised reply.

"Well," the officer explained, "neighbors have seen him alone in the mornings for far too long now, and have grown quite concerned that he must have lost his job and be in need."

"Oh, no," said my colleague's wife. "My husband doesn't work regular hours because he's a newspaper man."

This anecdote, I think, embraces several elements:

nosey neighbors, the traditional Japanese honor, common decency and concern for the next man, the importance of keeping the family unit strong — and the somewhat annoying fact that unless you are going to work on a jam-packed train each morning — and wearing a suit and tie in the process — you cannot possibly be working in the accepted sense of the word.

So Japan is kind. But it can also be downright unfair.

Some time ago, a young woman editor told me that her mother, who worked as a typist in a bank, wanted to be a teller but wasn't considered good looking enough.

"Doesn't that annoy you?" I asked her. I mean, if a company ever denied my dear old mother an opportunity, a promotion, on the basis of her looks and not her intelligence or general competence, I'd be in to see the management in no time at all."

"Well," the editor shrugged, seemingly impervious to the problem, "it isn't right, I know, treating my mother like that. But... well, it's the system. That's the way it's done in Japan."

What has since both annoyed and amazed me is that this young editor accepted this nonsense and wasn't even moved to write about it. It neither surprised nor infuriated her enough. Happily, such reticence does not apply to another Japanese editor. He can't wait to confront the system and probably will one day, when he gets mad enough. He surprised me the other day by saying that Japan was being manipulated, ruled, bled, and suppressed by a mere handful of companies, which he blamed for his "life in hell." He spoke about Tokyo's high rents, and the exorbitant cost of food, clothes, and services. "One day," he said, "I will get out."

An apology rights virtually any wrong in Japan. It always has. Annoy Immigration officials and they will await your written admission of guilt, then forgive you. Upset the managing editor at this newspaper, and he will expect the same.

It was against this kind of backdrop that two of my colleague editors, both of them highly competent, were obliged to confess that *The Weekly* rolled off the presses bearing an incorrect date. Unless the error had been spotted — as it was, by an alert proof reader — there would have been two May 19 editions instead of only one. The error was immediately corrected, the paper was reprinted. The following day, my colleagues sat down to admit the misdemeanour — even though it was not entirely their fault.

It will never happen again, they said. But they are wrong. It will, of course, though not necessarily during their tenure, because, like you and me, they are human.

Finally, there is the letter from the reader, a Roman Catholic priest, about my column that found me "Really Coffee Mad!" If I want a cheap cup of coffee, the priest tells me, I should drop by his parish hall.

"We have good, free Columbian coffee for everybody," he says. Then he adds, "If you want an expensive coffee, may I suggest you go to Nagoya and pay ¥50,000 for it."

A friend was amused by this thought. Those people who are stupid enough to pay ¥50,000 for a coffee, she said, were doubtless the same ones who rented time in a solid gold bath — by the minute!

Only in Japan. Only in Japan.

Teaching the Japanese English

SOON AFTER ARRIVING in Tokyo in October 1989, I applied for my first job — as an English teacher. "Nearly all Westerners who stay in Japan teach English," a colleague writer had told me. "It's the quickest way to cope with astronomical prices." It is. But for me, there were initial difficulties, and, mounting the steep, narrow steps to a language school in the Tokyo suburb of Toshimaen — having taken three trains and walked for 20 minutes to get there — I was to face them uncompromisingly.

The school had advertised for "an experienced native English speaker" to teach 10 hours each week. Since the students would be teens and businessmen, I felt I was eminently qualified to tutor them. Twenty of my 33 years as a journalist-author (10 published books and some 500 magazines pieces) have been spent teaching my language. At one point, I was a professor of written English, and of English as a second language, at the University of Montreal. But all this was to little avail.

"Your resume is impressive," said the woman who interviewed me, "but you're English, aren't you? And you're over twenty-nine."

"Yes," I said. "I am both of those — and experienced."

"Unfortunately," the woman went on, "we're looking for a younger person with an American accent."

This kind of discrimination, I discovered, is seething and it confronts all too many foreign teachers in Japan. The country has become so preoccupied with learning English that it has distorted its sense of judgment and fair play. In truth, the woman would not have known an American accent if she had heard one. Or an Australian or New Zealand one, come to that.

Competition for good teaching jobs in Japan is high. Each year, its Immigration Bureau issues some 2,000 work visas to foreign language teachers who mostly find jobs in the eighty-seven schools that are officially recognized by Japan's Ministry of Education. In reality, however, the great rush to teach — and to learn — is much more dramatic. Estimates of the number of language, or conversation schools run as high as 9,000 and, according to some of them, 70,000 foreigners are teaching English at any given time in Tokyo alone, nearly all of them on three-month tourist visas — people who have never taught in their lives before. This, then, supports an irony: that in their irrepressible enthusiasm to learn English, tens of thousands of Japanese have allowed themselves to be taught by unqualified people who happen to merrily look or sound good. As a manager in a school sponsored by a top Tokyo department store explained, "We hire teachers the students will find cute and relate to."

By that reckoning, appear smart, young and happy, and hail either from the United States or Britain, and you will get a job in days. Look over 50, fed up and tired with job hunting and listening to all this non-sensical discrimination, and it may take weeks — as I found out — regardless of your nationality, or whether or not you know your subject well and can teach it thoroughly.

A young American I met in Ikebukuro, Tokyo, was walking testimony to discrimination, too. Five conversation schools had rejected him because he was not a woman. Two of these had turned down his New Zealand-born girlfriend because she was not a blonde.

Nor was my wife spared the indignity. On sabbatical from her job as the principal of a busy public school in Montreal, Canada — and an expert in teaching English as both a first and a second language — she was dismayed to be told that one Tokyo employer was refusing to hire her because he earnestly sought a man. On another occasion, when she applied to teach French to a group of Hitachi company executives who were planning a trip to Paris, she was passed over because it was wrongly assumed that because she worked in Canada, she necessarily spoke Canadian French instead of European French. Born in Egypt, my wife was educated entirely in the French system. French is her mother tongue, and she speaks it to perfection.

Without even looking at her resume, one school — the Gregg Institute — insisted on testing her English grammar and syntax. Comprised entirely of multiple-choice questions, the test was highly insulting to an experienced English educator. The management later offered my wife a contract, but to this day she remains perplexed by the enormous breadth of the topic of an essay she was given a few minutes to write — "My outlook on education."

To be fair, Gregg cares about who will teach its

students while many other schools don't, viewing the teaching of English purely as a business. Professional teachers call these institutions "factories." I term them "sausage machines," and find it odious that they should even presume to question the qualified.

At yet another school, I recall, I was invited to watch how teaching the Japanese should, ideally, be done. My tutor: a young man of 23 from Oregon who, before settling in Japan had worked in a warehouse. In Tokyo, he worked as an English conversation teacher — with a fake degree, and with very little knowledge of how the language works. Needless to say, his teaching was abominable and I watched him in some dismay for three minutes before departing.

Then there was the school manager — a young American who had been a carpet salesman in Detroit — who told me, "After observing two of your classes, you will be required to give one yourself as a sort of audition, without payment." I was not pleased.

"Have you ever met a benevolent plumber who fixes pipes for nothing?" I asked him.

"No," he replied, "I can't say that I have."

"Well, I don't teach for nothing."

Like many other language schools in Japan, this one hired virtually anyone, fake degree and all, and espoused the theory that the student should be exposed to as many English teachers and accents as possible. Experienced professors the world over, however, have long thought differently about teaching. Absolutely integral to all good tutoring is a professor-student relationship that is built with time. In Asia, acute cultural differences dictate that this relationship be built on trust as well.

As the weeks rolled on, I was heartened to find language school administrators who also felt this way, and who appreciated my worth. Long before asking my nationality and age — which schools do to everyone — they inquired about my teaching credentials and visa. One was The Japan Times Language School, run by professionals. Others were Executive Education, the Cambridge English School, which is affiliated to the British Council, the British Broadcasting Corporation, and Cambridge University — and the Tokyo Foreign Language College, where my wife is now happily working. In fact, the college engaged me to replace an absent teacher and I enjoyed the two-week assignment immensely.

When it was over, however, and with my travel funds dwindling, I was grateful when I received an urgent call one Friday night to fill in for an ailing Australian teacher at a little school in Shimo-Akatsuka, but was saddened by what I saw there. Alas it happens too often in Japan.

At precisely 5 p.m., the owner opened the classroom door, led in five or six small children, and announced, "Twenty-minutes, please. Give them verbs."

He then introduced me to a second class of youngsters — "another 20 minutes, please. This time, nouns."

Next came a dentist's wife whom I recalled having taught elsewhere, and I was more than pleased to see her. She seemed less nervous than she had before, and did not address the carpet.

"What . . . did . . . you . . . do . . . today?" I began, as I so often did in those perplexing days.

"I cook," the woman said. "I cook lice in my chicken."

"In your what?" I asked.

"In my kitchen," came the corrected reply.

I smiled. Although the woman felt sufficiently comfortable to start building sentences, the occasion remained distinctly unsatisfying for me. In her nine years at that school, she confided, she had been processed by nearly 100 different teachers. On my way home that night, I thought what her progress might have been had she been taught by one or two. But that, it seems, is how it is in Japan. So long as foreigners are hired to entertain instead of teach, and experienced teachers are so often left unrecognized, the country will be poorer.

"I feel sorry for the Japanese," my wife mused ruefully as we reflected on an education system that is administered by clerks, and certainly not by educators. "They really should get an awful lot more for their money."

They should, indeed. But until all schools are licensed, and standards closely monitored, the sad truth is that they probably won't. Teaching English will continue to be show business, and all those thousands of Japanese who really want to learn English will go on renting foreigners by the hour, without knowing better — just to hear them speak.

Linda's Luck

THIS IS A STORY OF honesty, sheer good luck, and unbelievable initiative. My friend Linda K., a carefree Californian, cycled the 10 km from Iogi to Kichijoji to start a heavy day's teaching for Berlitz. No sooner had she arrived there, however, than she was on the telephone. "I've lost my bag," she said. "It's got *everything* in it!"

This, it seems, happens quite a lot here. Foreigners are dunderheads. They'd lose their feet if they weren't somehow attached to their bodies. Some of them suspect, automatically that because they are in Japan anything they lose will be returned.

Linda K. wanted me to cycle around the neighborhood to see where the black, leather bag may have tumbled from her bicycle.

"D'you mean to tell me you didn't secure it?" I said to her.

"No," she said. "I left in a hurry and cycled off with it balancing on the back."

There was one thing in her favor. She lived in Japan.

"Well," I said to lift her spirits, "because you're living in Japan the chances are very good that you'll get your bag back. In fact, they are excellent."

"I hope so. God, I hope so," said Linda K.

True to my prediction, when the phone rang again about an hour or so later, it was a man named Daisuke

Takakawa, a young Japanese on holiday in Tokyo from his job as a corporate solicitor in London, calling to say that the bag was in his hands. While on her way to work, his mother had spotted it atop a heap of garbage and had taken it to the local police box only to find it closed. "It looked too good to be there," she told her son when she took it home.

"What, the garbage?" he asked.

"No, the bag," his mother replied. "It's a very nice one."

Daisuke Takakawa searched its contents, found a telephone number, and dialed it immediately.

That's when I came into the picture.

Linda's luck was that her bag had been spotted by a woman with a keen eye for good things. Her next bit of good fortune was that both spoke superb English and, having ascertained that the bag belonged to a foreigner, felt totally comfortable about phoning. Linda was lucky, too — *very* lucky — that the garbage truck had started its rounds a little later than usual that day.

Some questions, however, have since sprung to my mind: How does a lost item that is so obviously expensive end up on the garbage? It is well known that the Japanese freely discard what other people consider well worth hanging on to; anything seen in the street — how good a condition it might be in — must either have been left there on purpose or fallen from the back of a truck.

And why didn't the person who picked the bag from the sidewalk and cast it away so readily — the first person to touch it after it had fallen from the bicycle — show some sort of judgment and, like Takakawa and his mother, open it. Fortunately for Linda, the Takakawas showed a lot of initiative.

At 10.30 a.m. that very day, I fitted the face to the voice I had heard on the telephone. I met Daisuke Takakawa at Iogi Station and, as promised, he brought the bag. He was 27, athletic and trim, and wore a T-shirt and shorts. "When a woman loses her purse," he said, "she loses herself." His English was so good that I thought he was a thoroughbred Englishman, and what he said was true indeed.

Later, and finally home after several tiring classes, my friend Linda checked the contents of her bag. Sure enough, everything was there —her designer watch, a little snap-fastener purse containing a ¥5,000-note and about ¥1,000 in loose change, her sun glasses, a walletful of bank cards, her ward card in a separate case, two packets of tissue paper she'd doubtlessly been handed outside Shinjuku Station, a pink, plastic makeup bag, a white comb, a tin of fruit candies, and one or two unmentionables.

Have I missed anything?

Oh, yes. The only thing Linda *didn't* get back when she lost her bag was the tuna and lettuce sandwich she'd packed for her lunch. Strange? Not at all. I am very partial to lettuce and tuna sandwiches, especially when they are made with fresh, brown bread. And anyway, besides being exceedingly hungry by this time, who else would have wanted to eat a sandwich that had spent time on a pile of garbage near a supermarket in Iogi? Only me.

Next time Linda K. loses her bag I would like it to contain a loaf of French bread, a hefty chunk of Stilton cheese, and a little bottle of Port wine. We will need the wine to drink to the honesty of Japan.

Struggling together

ONE OF THE MOST REVEALING things about Japan is in all those people who are essentially doing the same thing as yourself — enjoying the culture while broadening personal horizons. In this respect, the 15-year-old daughter, Nathalie, my wife and I brought with us is having the kind of education no school ever gives.

My family and I live in a foreigners' house. So do a cluster of Australians, Americans, and Canadians, not to mention a handful of Brits, of which I am one, even though I have homes both in Canada and the United States. The education for our daughter, Nathalie, is in what these people say about me, each other, and Japan, and how they adapt to the Japanese way of life.

The Aussie's — "G'day, mate!" — are not only easily identified by the way they speak, but by what they eat. At breakfast, they paste onto thick slices of toast a dark, brown vegetable extract known as Vegemite. During World War II, the British government issued — ration-free — a similar product. Marmite, as it is still called, is credited with pumping the most important vitamins into an entire generation of the nation's youngest people, when they needed vitamins most.

The Americans, meanwhile, are peanut butter crazy, the Canadians don't appear to eat anything unusual —

if at all — and the British, even the fittest among them, have long since abandoned Marmite for eggs and bacon.

At nights, the Brits are quieter than the Aussie's, who are quieter than the Americans, who are as noisy as hell — especially when they remember how the Japanese are buying up their country, which may not actually be true. According to *Megatrends 2000*, co-authored by John Naisbitt and Patricia Aburdene (both Americans by the way), "of the total direct foreign investment in the United States — $250 billion at the end of 1987 — the British held the biggest share with 28 percent, followed by the Dutch with 21 percent and the Japanese with only 12 percent."

Nonetheless, Americans staying in Japan *do* have a legitimate beef when it comes to dealing with Immigration. Until they are successful in getting a working visas, they must leave the country every three months, while the Brits, the Canadians, the Aussies, and the few New Zealanders — or Kiwis — I bump into from time to time, don't.

Unfair? Of course it is. So is the world. Politicians might not like each other and, in so doing, pass on their frustrations to ordinary people.

In the foreigners' house, I'm pleased to report, the people get along well, despite the politicians. Only the other morning, I saw a Brit frying eggs for a Canadian, a generous American inviting a New Zealander to dip into his peanut butter, and an Aussie donating a jar of Vegemite to a French woman from New Caledonia, about which most of the residents had hitherto heard absolutely nothing. Predictably, the woman thought that Vegemite was the worst thing for the gullet since cough mixture was invented.

The education? When spirits sag, people of all backgrounds pull together — the Vegemites, the Brits, the Canadians, the Americans, and anyone else who might be around.

But there is more. The other night, Nathalie admitted she had never encountered an Australian, and didn't know what one sounded like until she saw the movie *Crocodile Dundee*. A young Mexican woman, meanwhile, who works at her embassy, and who acted as secretary to Mexico's president during his visit to Japan, confessed to not having ever seen snow until it adorned Tokyo earlier this year. And the New Caledonia woman finally confessed to me, but not to the Aussie's, that she actually hated Vegemite.

Most of us live in the foreigners' house, by the way, because — as honorable as we are — we cannot find enough landlords who are prepared to rent us apartments. If and when we do, they want us to pay two months' rent as a deposit, plus the real estate agent's fee, and another hefty chunk of cash — almost always the equivalent of another two months' rent. While the Japanese pay this without questioning it, Westerners most definitely don't. We find key money abhorrent because in most civilized countries it is illegal under criminal law.

So, while we enjoy Japan's cultural life, we are making the best of a country that has many hardships. And we are doing it at much greater odds than a lot of Japanese people give us credit for. Those hardships, I believe — the low standard of living that has been inflicted by such a wealthy nation on its people, not to mention a dreadfully poor quality of life — are the very things that have kept us foreigners together.

Out of our struggle to survive here, some of us have forged friendships that could well last a life-time.

Unlearning racism

WHEN I WAS A SMALL BOY growing up in London, I learned — from my school, and my uncles and aunts, no less — that people who looked or sounded different were just that. They were *different.* They were foreigners. They were aliens. They were outsiders. And, as such, they had to be told to stay their distance and be discriminated against, because they could not possibly deserve the same rights as a native-born person. Of course, there was a war on then and, in a meager defense, it could be said that things were different. Nonetheless, I spent much of my 54th birthday telling myself how lucky I was to have been inspired over the past 40 years to unlearn this infernal nonsense.

Today, racism is absolutely repugnant to me. I can think of nothing I dislike more. Racism, after all, comes about when one group decides that it is better, more gifted, more intelligent, cleaner, more honorable and hence more acceptable, than another. It is based on vanity, self-grandeur, bigotry, stupidity, a lack of knowledge, and blatant inhumanity. And this brings me to the Japanese.

No one can condone what the Americans and the Canadians did to them during the war that raged when I was growing up. By confiscating Japanese businesses and interning the innocent people who both started and patronized them — those who looked different and spoke another language hardly anyone in America or Canada could ever hope to understand — they were perpetuating racism of the worst possible kind. They were labeling Japanese immigrants as aliens simply because they didn't understand them and assumed, wrongly, of course, that they could not be trusted.

Similarly, no one can condone what the Japanese have been doing to their Korean and Chinese immigrants — exploiting them for their sweat while refusing to give them status, even a vote. In fact, in many ways, what the Japanese are doing to foreigners in *their* country is unprecedented. Today, there is no war to worry about, and there is not likely to be one. Yet the racism seems endless.

It seems absolutely preposterous to me, for instance, that Koreans and Chinese should have to assume Japanese names so as to hide their nationalities — just in case their neighbors find out who they *really* are and felt the urge to victimize them. It seems preposterous that after all these years, when Japan is trying to "internationalize," that it should be behaving in this way. It saddens me.

One of my new-found friends in Tokyo is a young Chinese woman who is married to a Japanese, and who can only find menial jobs — despite passing through a British education system in her native Hong Kong with honors. She speaks standard English infinitely better than most Americans I know, and could doubtless teach it more vigorously, too.

If I owned a language school and wanted someone to reach the Japanese students on their level, at their pace, and who had a profound knowledge of their language and their culture, I would hire her — immediately. But no one else in Tokyo will, it seems. After all, she *is* Chinese. But then, as someone shrewdly pointed out the other day, "How can you expect Japan to stop discriminating against other people when it hasn't yet stopped discriminating against its own people?"

What an amazing paradox from a country that oozes gentility, generosity, and civility.

Oh, by the way, I almost forgot to tell you. I unlearned racism by getting out of my own backyard 30 years ago. I traveled, met and worked with people of all denominations and from many parts of the world, knowing and liking them in the process. I can't think of a better way of doing it. The so-called "other people" I got to admire and love were the ones who, in their own quiet way, inspired me to understand that the world was not just for me, and never had been. The world, they helped me discover, was a mosaic of different nationalities, each one contributing something to the cause of mankind.

I would like the Japanese to discover this, too. They should. They are treated far better in the West than they treat Westerners here. Although their country still has a long way to go in these matters itself, the West is showing it how to combat racism — by example. Perhaps Japan should sit up and listen.

My man Taishi

NOW IT ALL MAKES SENSE — all those long days searching for a printer for my IBM-compatible computer when I was shrugged aside with a cursory "no stock." And all those occasions when, gasping for a Snicker's, I was told simply, "Not available." It all makes *perfect* sense, and I would like to tell you why and how.

First, I have heard it said — and you probably have, too — that Japan was born the day a group of Buddhists came careening down from Heaven, long before the Inquisition, long before Christ, even. The Buddhists feuded a bit, then settled back to run their country.

Out of all this, in about 604, a young Prince Regent named Shotoku Taishi exercised his talents as a religious, statesmanlike and artistic genius of the highest order. He compared Shinto to the root, Confucianism to the truck, and Buddhism to the fruit — all of the same tree.

I first came upon this illustrious man while browsing through an old bookstore and flipping the pages of a dusty volume that had been written in English about the time the Americans rewrote Japan's Constitution just after World War II. When I mentioned him to a group of students a day or so later, however, they knew little about him, except that his face had once adorned the former ¥10,000 note. Yet Taishi was worth considerably more than this.

After the ingenious story of Japan's creation, with its countless gods, whose ghostly lives continue to pursue the people to this very day, comes Taishi's *Seventeen Articles* on which the country's patriarchal system is unquestionably based. Read some of these sometime, and you will understand, among many other things, why the Japanese respect age, why they spend more than half their lives at the office, and why they are so efficient and honest. You'll also understand about *wa*:

> *Harmony* (wa) *is the highest. Non-rebelliousness of those below against those above, and those above against those below, this is what matters.*

This is an example of how old Taishi expressed himself. It is also an example of how he expected his fellow countrymen to behave. Of course, they followed this simple philosophy to the letter, and, at times overdid it. And this brings me back to the IBM-compatible printer and those Snicker's.

It took me quite some time to finally discover that to preserve the wa, the Japanese prefer never to say "no." It is disconcerting, but true. In America or Britain, a dealer would say, "No, Sir. I don't stock IBM printers. But if you go across the road they have dozens of them." Or if, while in New York City, you popped into a shop that sold only newspapers to buy a Snicker's, the clerk would be likely to say, "What the hell d'you think I want with chocolate, for chrissakes?"

"You mean, you don't sell chocolate?"

"No!"

In Japan, where people are much more civil, instead

of saying, "No, we don't sell IBM printers," they will usually say, "No stock," which implies that they sometimes have what you want, but not on that particular day. In the same way, when the man at the candy kiosk says "Not available" when you ask for Snicker's, he is somehow implying that he will never handle a Snicker's again in his life.

Other words substituted for a direct "no" include "maybe," "probably," "sometimes," "could be," and "so-so," which has finally found its way into Japanese-English dictionaries.

Anyway, my point is this: that old Taishi should have thought of all this. He should have realized just how many problems would be caused — in the name of wa — by his people not being able to say a simple "no." I wish I had met him. I would have told him this, nicely, of course, because he was a very young man.

He was always young, in fact, dying when he was only 28 years old. But just think of the impact he had. Today, 124 million Japanese think that saying no is rude, vulgar, too strong, too emphatic, too impolite, or, in the words of one of my former students, "too black and white."

I think Shotoku Taishi would have drunk to that.

The racist foreigners

STAND BY FOR THE DISQUIETING realization that too many Westerners living in Japan — themselves victims of Japanese racism and job discrimination — are helping to perpetuate these horrible vices. It reared up when a Californian woman phoned to ask me if, by chance, I knew an experienced teacher who could give two weeks of intensive English conversation lessons at short notice. Of course I knew one. An amiable and experienced high school teacher from Brisbane, Australia, who has just begun the unenviable task of looking for work here.

"No, no, no," the woman said quickly, "we have to have a native-speaking American."

"Well, if that's the way you feel," I said, "I want nothing to do with helping you find a teacher."

"It's not me," said the woman, "it's the Japanese owners. You know what a superficial society this is."

"Yes," I said quickly, "I do. But I don't bloodywell have to be part of it!"

Given this scenario, I salute those schools that have hired teachers from all denominations and ethnic backgrounds, most notably the Tokyo Foreign Language College and a little school in Shin-Okubo that is run by a Roman Catholic priest.

The priest was one of the first school administrators in Tokyo who dared to hire a black, but not without some initial difficulties. When neighborhood parents discovered their children were about to be taught by a Sri Lankan, they complained, And the priest — God bless his soul — stuck his hand in his pocket and offered them their money back.

"That man is staying right where he is," he said. And he did. The teacher, who speaks exquisite English, became a mainstay at the school for more than 12 years.

I cannot, however, condone the actions of the Westerner who gave a young Korean woman, known only as "Ms. Kim," the first direct discrimination she had ever experienced. It was ironic, indeed. Kim had answered an advertisement for a part-time telephone teaching position with everything a prospective employer could have asked for — plenty of experience, a working visa, and a heart-felt desire to stay in Japan for more than a year. Her conversation went smoothly until she was asked, "What is your nationality?"

Let Kim tell the story:

"After hearing that I was an American, born in Korea to Korean parents and had emigrated to the United States when I was four, the person at the other end of the phone went from being a competent English speaker to a helpless, stuttering fool. Obviously I had sounded blonde-haired and blue-eyed, and he felt cheated."

Was the Westerner who was running this school for his Japanese bosses looking for a native speaker? Of course he was. But he also told Kim that he really sought a "pure American."

God knows what a pure American is! At any rate, back in the United States, or in Britain or Australia, this preposterous little upstart would have faced a lawsuit for his actions. So would the silly Australian woman at the Roppongi branch of a school called ASA. She told an American that she had to teach in both high-heeled shoes and make-up, notwithstanding that by all reports, the American woman is far better looking without anything on her face than her female boss is with. But this is a slightly different matter.

Back to Kim. Being sharp and about eight times more intelligent than her interviewer, she said, "Ah, then, if you are looking for a pure American, you must be wanting an American Indian."

The comment went completely over the man's head.

"Perhaps," she reflects despondently, "if his students couldn't hear the 'Caucasianism' in my voice, they would demand a refund."

And she adds, "When will the Japanese learn that America is not a large, white melting pot, but a multi-colored one which includes Asian and black Americans? Or perhaps, as an 'unpure American,' it is not mine to question when and why."

She raises the all-important point, of course — that if the Japanese don't know all this, then we must teach them, even though they may be our employers. In years to come, when they have been *truly* "internationalized," they will surely be grateful to us for it.

Meanwhile, those Westerners who are echoing these vile sentiments on behalf of Japanese bosses, are racists themselves. They have a long way to go before they win my respect.

Tying up loose ends

REMEMBER THE TIME my colleague editor Big Mike Millard took me to his favorite Shinjuku coffee house and all the customers were either reading the newspaper or asleep? Remember how I felt when I had to pay ¥800 for a coffee, or, rather, *half* a cup of coffee? Well, my friend the Roman Catholic priest in Shin-Okubo, who has carved a little hobby out of doing useful research for me, has sent me more relevant information. He is surprised to find out, even though he has been in Tokyo for nearly 40 years, that the city's coffee houses are actually disappearing. In 1982, for example, Tokyo had 20,216 of them. Last year, it had only 12,654.

Reason? The owner of one such place, Fukuzo Shimizu, who also happens to be the director of the Tokyo Coffee Shop Owners' Union, says that the price of a cup of coffee in his Shinjuku establishment has risen 833 percent since 1955 while, over the same period, the price of land in the neighborhood has shot up 20,570 percent!

But that is not all. The coffee shops are also victims of the current labor shortage. Ideally, says Shimizu, labor costs for all workers should add up to between 30 and 35 percent of gross sales, and no more. But, with part-time wages rising all over the Tokyo area as businesses earnestly try to attract workers from other parts of Japan, a simple profit in a coffee shop is now almost impossible unless it sells sandwiches, cakes, or desserts.

Now, both soaring land prices and the high cost of labor threaten to push a cup of coffee far beyond what the average well-paid office worker is prepared to pay. So more shops, especially those that have a large coffee-only clientele, are expected to go out of business. "Instead of struggling to sell enough coffees for between ¥400 and ¥500 each," Shimizu adds, "it's much easier and beneficial for coffee shop owners to lease their commercial space and make money that way. That's what many of them have decided to do."

That's all right by me. I'm happy to drop into Doutor every morning for my ¥180-coffee. And I know Big Mike is happy with all *three* of his!

Talking of high prices, are the Japanese aware that to have a pair of shoes repaired here costs almost as much as a new pair in North America? I faced this reality this week. Well, almost. When I took my favorite slip-ons into Mister Minit in Ogikubo, I was horrified to discover that a new sole would cost ¥2,150, and a heel ¥1,900 — roughly $35 Canadian. I bought the shoes in Plattsburgh, New York, for $40 (U.S.)

Should I have them repaired again? Or should I toss them away? I will probably opt for the former. I get attached to old things — old jackets, old shirts, and yes, old shoes. Just before coming to Japan last October, I reluctantly cast off a pair of brogues I had worn for 25 years.

Finally, every so often I have to clear my desk and rid my intray of all the little slips of paper, many of them suggestions for my column that come from people who either want to shake my hand or ring my neck. This week is such an occasion:

> *Dear Mr. Waller, you are better when you write humor. Why not every week?*

Answer: Because humor is bloody hard to write, and I don't feel in a humorous mood every week to do it — especially having to cope with Big Mike and some of the very stupid things that happen around here.

> *Dear Mr. Waller, why are you always bashing Japan?*

There is a simple philosophy about which a group called The Inkspots used to sing — "You always hurt the one you love." But I do not bash Japan. Japan bashes me. I pay more in income tax here than a lot of people earn. And yet, I have no rights.

> *Dear Mr. Waller: I really love your columns, in fact, I adore them. But with reference to some of them, who cares about your love of socks, the price of coffee, and Big Mike?*

Answer: I do. Given a choice between Big Mike and a cup of Doutor coffee, I'd have to take the coffee. Given a choice between coffee and socks, I'd think of my feet first.

Voices in a house of foreigners

IT IS FAST APPROACHING 11 p.m., and, in a little suburban street in Nerima-ku, the white-frame house is hushed, its curtains drawn, its porch light twinkling against the cold, black night. The only sign of life in the wood-paneled living room is Mr. Henry, a white-bearded curmudgeon who exists in a pall of pipe smoke. He breaks the silence.

"I got a ticket on my bicycle today," he says tragically, "and I wish I could read it. In fact, I'd give *anything* to be able to read it. One of these days, I'd like to wake up to read every notice and sign in Tokyo, and what people are saying to each other on the subway. They may be talking about me!"

The house is occupied exclusively by foreigners, 29 in all, and most of them, like Mr. Henry, are English teachers. Among the others are a big American businessman, a rangy Canadian girl with a head of black, dancing curls who sings in a club, a wide-eyed Mexican girl who works at her embassy, and a lean, introspective Scot with a deep accent who is studying Japanese.

"Who the hell's going to understand his Japanese?" quips Mr. Henry, spearing a potato and devouring it almost whole. "Hardly anyone here can understand his bloody English!"

If Mr. Henry can be said to live in a morose world

of reality in modern-day Japan, one of the other guests very definitely dwells in a somewhat metaphysical world of dreams and innocent ideals. Elliot is a New York City-born Buddhist who chants in his room five time a day, and whose prized possessions are a Water Pik and a beige, canvas bag from which he is absolutely inseparable. Mr. Henry has noted that Elliot actually takes the bag to the washroom and surmises that it may contain the Crown Jewels.

Life in the house, and the characters who make it different from all others in this corner of suburban Tokyo, may come and go by the hour, according to their line of duty. Shortly after 11:30 p.m., the latecomers arrive home from their dates, their gallivanting, and their teaching. Some, particularly those whose tight budgets prohibit them from buying too much good food, have traveled two hours by train and another 10 minutes by bicycle from Iogi Station, to earn a measly ¥5,000. Others, who have been in Japan several months, and who have respectable bank accounts to show for it, have found more lucrative evening work in Shinjuku, a 20-minute train ride away.

"If ever there was a graveyard shift," says Mr. Henry, still munching, "it's this one. If you don't die of boredom, some motorist will probably slam into you when you're riding your bike back in the goddam dark!"

Most of the inhabitants in this princely house of *gaijin* are not as fatalistic or disillusioned as Mr. Henry. They are in Japan to savour its culture and earn money doing it. One, a 22-year-old who has found himself a Japanese girlfriend, wants to save enough for a deposit on a house back in his native England. Another, Esme, a spirituous, loud-talking New-Yorker who is always so confidently naked of make-up, merely wants to support herself as well as she can as a language teacher so she can stay in Tokyo to study calligraphy. She has adapted to her new life with gay resolute.

"Everything in a culture is relative," she says with a shrug. "So they spit in Japan. So they work too hard. So what? So they behave like tigers on the subway, get drunk, and are quite happy to bribe the landlord by paying him key money. In New York they kill each other."

"Quite so," says Mr. Henry, sucking philosophically as he applies a little flicker of flame to his pipe. "Quite so. But at least in New York they talk to each other and don't fall asleep on the subway."

"Anyone who falls asleep on the Manhattan subway," Esme counters in a shrill voice, "wakes up to find his wallet gone! That's why New Yorkers stay awake."

Almost the same conversation has gone on in the guest house every day and night since Yoshikazu Yaji, 38, opened it on a hot day in August 1989 as a home-away-from-home for any foreigner who could afford the average monthly rent of ¥55,000 to stay there. Predictably, guests have piled in from almost every corner of the world, mostly Australia, the United States, Canada and Britain. But while his motives were commercial, Mr. Yaji's heart remains big, soft, and open. So, unlike most landlords, he is unusually compassionate, and is both respected and loved as a friend. "It's not just the sake he sends over," guests say. "It's the things he does for us without us having to ask him."

They remember Mr. Yaji's gifts of cakes, the

smoking room they asked for and got, the odd party he has thrown in their honor, the extra table or chair he has installed in a room, and the times he has taken those who were luggage-bound to Iogi Station to save them a cab fare. Not long ago, some of the guests decided that if they didn't like each other's cooking smells, or the way they left their washing-up undone, they nonetheless had something in common. They were movie lovers. When Yoshikazu Yaji heard about it — that very week — he installed a VCR in the lounge.

It is now shortly after midnight, and Mr. Henry shambles off to bed grumbling. There are elements of communal living he doesn't much care for — having to store his food in plastic bags that are crammed into a corner of the lounge by any one of the three bulky fridges. Sometimes he forgets where he has put his cheese and can't find his yogurt. So he borrows Elliot's. It has also been known for guests to borrow Mr. Henry's teapot without washing it afterwards, take his umbrella, hide his shoes, and eat his bananas.

Mr. Henry is also tired of having to take a shower by squatting on a little green, plastic stall under a faint spray of water, and of rolling out his futon night after night, let alone stirring on mornings so spitefully cold they make your breath stand still. "If I want to freeze to death," he says, "I'll move to Siberia. If I want a life on the floor, I'll join the Boy Scouts. And if I want nagging about any of my views, I'll go back to my wife."

Later that night, some of the second-floor guests who want to sleep can hardly believe their ears — an inane conversation that is more appropriate to the lounge. As Mr. Henry stretches on his futon, he responds to a knock on his door.

"How much does it cost you to run your electric blanket?" Elliot inquires in a voice so loud it echoes along the corridor.

"What?" says Mr. Henry, perplexed.

"Your electric blanket," says Elliot. He is standing there like a fire hydrant in spectacles. "What are your electricity bills like?"

Mr. Henry tells Elliot that he neither knows nor cares, and is willing to pay almost anything to spend a warm night in Japan. He couldn't care less about bottomless cups of coffee and smoked meat on rye sandwiches, both commonplace in his native Canada, but his comfort is something he will never compromise.

"Oh, I agree," says Elliot. "In fact, I couldn't agree more. That's why, as soon as I get paid, I'm buying an electric blanket myself."

"Well," says Mr. Henry, "make sure you get the Toshiba. It's the best on the market. It heats up very quickly."

"That's good to know," says Elliot. "Very useful information. By the way, do you know how to fix the cuffs on pants?"

"Ask one of the women."

By this time it is nearly 1 a.m., and Mr. Henry wants to sleep. He does, leaving the late-night group watching an Arnold Schwarzenegger movie. He hates Arnold Schwarzenegger.

Rumor has that Mr. Yaji couldn't speak a single word

of English when he opened his foreigners' house, but that he learned it with courage and from a little white dictionary he carried in his back pocket. Why he should want to learn English is a mystery. He is a wealthy man, indeed, owning several acres of neighborhood land that is said to have been in his family for more than 800 years. Most of it has been built up now, with small houses and sheds, save for the cabbage patch to the west of the house, and a large vegetable garden across the road to the south.

It is also a mystery why a contented, tranquil man like Mr. Yaji would opt to deal with foreigners, many of whom can be noisy when they want to. He opened his house, he says, to diversify his interests. Besides this, he felt that a home full of foreigners, whom he likes and trusts, would be good for his neighbors. Now busy running the house — collecting the rents and incinerating the garbage to make compost for his vegetables, many of which he gives away — Mr. Yaji is a slim, affable, jean-clad man towering above neighborhood children who afford the foreigners the kind of reverence they would a friendly, extra-terrestrial being.

True to the Japanese work ethic, which says that the most menial of jobs must be done well, before opening his own institution he visited 20 similar ones to see if, and where, they had gone wrong. He would never admit it, for he is a humble man, but he strove to make his foreigners' home-away-from-home the very best there was.

"And I think he's done it. In fact, I know he has. Our Mr. Yaji is a very bright, kind man."

This voice belongs to Mr. Stanley, a small, round-faced Englishman who possesses a somewhat puckish air, and who has made Mr. Yaji's guest house his principal home.

People come, and people go. But Mr. Stanley says, "I'm in no hurry to move out."

The sun is shining. A new day has begun. The group that munches on hot toast in the living room is different from the one that was up half the night. With the exception of Mr. Henry, the early risers only ever see the late-nighters on weekends — unless, that is, someone falls asleep with a radio on.

"The thing is," says Mr. Henry, his glasses steaming up against the heat from the kerosene burner as he pokes two slices of bread into the toaster oven, "we need to get some organization around here. That lousy late night crowd didn't do all their washing up again, and there are peanuts on the floor!"

His words fall on deaf ears. A willowy New Zealand girl is reading the paper, a blonde from Minnesota is filing her nails, and Mr. Stanley has come in with his raincoat on. He was last spotted entering the men's shower room just a few minutes before, stripped to the waist. Now he stands ready to take on the world as a firm but fatherly teacher in a girls' private school near Ikebukuro. When he first moved in, he sported a Groucho Marx mustache. Since having it trimmed, he has begun to think he is Clarke Gable — just as the Australian men who lived under Mr. Yaji's roof have each considered himself a Crocodile Dundee.

"It makes you wonder, doesn't it?" Mr. Stanley begins, surveying the mess. "It makes you wonder how some people live at home."

"You'd better believe it," says Mr. Henry.

He cleans the sink and stacks away a pile of cups and plates — both despite a notice Mr. Yaji has stuck above the water heater:

Be sure to put into cupboard away your dishes.

It is an odd notice. So is the one posted on the refrigerator doors:

Please put into bread.

Or the one in each room:

Look At For Fire.

This quaint, courageous use of English, guests agree, has helped endear Mr. Yaji to them, making his a princely house of fellowship indeed. It was not so princely, however, the day he found too much washing up had been left undone and closed the kitchen until it had been cleared away. Nor was it such when, to the horror of all who lived there, a thief functioned in their midst. That was the morning Mr. Henry wrote a note declaring, "The Japanese don't steal, so why the hell should we?"

Visibly horrified, and suspecting the culprit, Mr. Yaji consulted his dictionary and scratched another little note:
Thief go out.
The thief eventually did, though not by choice. And,

with a chuckle of relief and embarrassment, Mr. Yaji vowed never to let a dishonorable person set foot on his property again.

So far as it is known, none has, and, to the delight of old stalwarts like Mr. Stanley and Mr. Henry, the place is now so safe that if anyone leaves a camera, wallet, address book, or phone card in the lounge overnight, it will be waiting for them in the morning.

"So," says Mr. Henry, "I'd better get dressed and get out of here. If I don't leave early, I don't find a seat on the train."

"You're worrying about a place on the train to *sit*," says Elliot, his voice rising. "I can't even find a place to *stand!*"

He departs. So does Mr. Stanley and those who were eating toast. And as they go, the cleaning staff arrives. Another day in the life of a foreigners' house is ending. Or, depending on whichever way you look at it, just beginning.

Nihonjin classroom

IF I HAVE LEARNED NOTHING else in 35 years of writing, I have certainly become aware that, more than anything else, people want to read about themselves — why they act the way they do, principally, and how others view them. This theory has been so well tried that it functions nicely as a writer's springboard for ideas. Tell people why they are like they are, and they will surely listen — particularly in Japan where the most often asked questions are, "Do you like Japanese food?" Or, "What do you think of Tokyo?"

So, when I delivered the keynote lecture at *The Japan Times'* 13th Annual English Seminar at Susono, on the slopes of Mount Fuji, a few weeks back, I felt it appropriate to tell an audience of nearly 100 participants something I thought they might not be fully aware of.

Whereas the typical American school or college has its share of weapons, drugs, violence, bad language, vandalism, graffiti, disinterest among its student body, as well as dishonesty and bitterness, the Japanese equivalent has virtually none. There is very little cheating in a classroom here, and discipline problems are overshadowed by an inordinate amount of respect — among the students, for the school, and for the teacher, however effective he or she may be.

Added to this, the Japanese have long believed that

learning — no matter how useless the subject — is eminently worthwhile.

This is the positive side of English teaching in Japan. There are also some other cultural problems which, to the unsuspecting, can make the job challenging, baffling, dispiriting, frustrating, and hard. There is, for instance, little or no teacher-student interaction. Young people seldom, if ever, raise their hands to ask questions or to debate a point of view fearing that doing so might undermine the teacher by interrupting the lesson or wasting time. Consequently, originality of thought or ideas is not apparent in the Japanese classroom, and nearly all students who study English there, tend to imitate each other — mistakes, and all — in the same manner.

The dangers of being perceived as "different," and ostracized as a result, are also very real, and it is against these that the experienced teacher toils to make students comfortable enough to express themselves. Essentially, she coaxes them to accept that such simple words as *what*, *why*, *how*, *when*, and *where* are absolutely integral to learning.

Students of all ages rarely respond to questions put to them as a group. For example, if while taking attendance the teacher asks if Yuko or Koji are absent, no one will respond. When the question is put to a specific student —"Makiko, are Yuko or Koji in school today?" — the results are almost always different.

Then, as the lesson progresses, students strive to maintain harmony at the expense of learning.

"Do you understand?" asks the teacher. But no one utters a single word or raises as much as a finger. That is, until the teachers gives an order —"Raise your hands if you understand." Usually, one student does, then another . . . and so on.

That is not all. When asked any sort of question, a student invariably consults his or her peers before answering. If this leads the instructor to believe that either the student doesn't know the answer, or is cheating, it shouldn't. The student is merely trying to seek approval — and is ensuring that if some sort of consensus has been reached, he or she will not break it.

Strangely, students who are complimented will quite often perform erratically — purposely — so they will not attract any further attention. The need for harmony, after all, is at the root of nearly everything the Japanese do, from kindergarten to the board room, where decisions are made by committee. In the classroom, "consensus harmony" is the students' oxygen.

So is sleep — in coffee shops, at the movies, on the trains, on park benches, even during lessons. In the West, of course, a student who takes a nap during a class session is immediately ejected for not paying attention. Seasoned teachers know, however, that when the Japanese sleep in class it is because they are genuinely tired from a rugged lifestyle about which they never complain.

Fortunately, no one slept during my lecture at Susono. In fact, when it was over, something unusual happened. The Japanese asked so many questions that the session ran an extra, unscheduled 20 minutes.

Whoever said that teaching English to the Japanese was easy? On the slopes of Mount Fuji, at least some of them came to understand just *where, why, how,* and *when* it isn't.

My big investment

I DON'T KNOW WHY I chose to entrust my business to the Aoyama branch of the mighty Fuji Bank shortly after arriving in Tokyo, except that it was there when I was. On an impulse, I sauntered in, looked timidly around at all the people there, and seated myself before an attractive young clerk whose job it was to help people open bank accounts. From then on, the forms seemed to flow back and forth unceasingly, and each time I completed one — name, address, phone number, age — the clerk dabbed a little red mark on it with her *hanko*.

"So, that's it," I said to her finally. "I now have a Japanese bank account."

"No, no, no," she said, "You have to pay some money."

"Money? What for?"

"To open the account with."

I pressed a ¥100 coin into her soft, white hand. It was a process that invited more papers. When I opened an account in Florida the teller asked me for my mother's middle name, and I couldn't for the life of me remember it. Then she asked me what her maiden name was. "God knows," I said. "I never really knew my mother when she was a maiden."

In Japan, bankers want customers to protect their investments with secret codes — sets of numbers that must often be conceived on the spot. Predictably, I thought of the day, month, and year of my birth, then the last four digits of my phone number, and wrote them down. Again, the woman applied her hanko, then disappeared with my ¥100 coin on a green plastic tray.

That, I surmised, was the end of it. When she returned, however, she did so with more papers to sign. And when I had finished these — and was feeling more and more like Tokyo's newest tycoon — I was suddenly overtaken by a wicked idea.

"You realize," I said, deadly serious, "that this is the most important money your bank has ever been entrusted with?"

The clerk's eyes narrowed and she looked at me painfully perplexed, as if she had done something dreadfully wrong. She handed me my bankbook. I checked my balance. Sure enough, the ¥100 yen had been deposited.

"If I withdraw my money," I continued blithely, "the entire Tokyo Stock exchange will enter an irreversible spin, and Japan will grind to a standstill in minutes."

"Withdraw your money and stand still?" the clerk repeated quizzically.

I nodded.

At this, the woman hurriedly fetched an assistant manager, a grave, calm fellow who looked as if he'd been sent to Fuji Bank by his wife, to get him out of the way while she did the washing. I sat nervously before him, not knowing what he was saying or thinking. By this time, the rest of the staff had stopped working to look at me. I did my utmost to remain rational.

"Without my money," I repeated, "it will be impossible for your bank or your country to carry on."

Obviously not amused, the assistant manager rolled

his eyes and loped off to call the manager. A short, wiry man, he sprang into service immediately.

"May I help you?" he inquired gravely, in an excessively polite accent he probably uses for perpetual complainers.

"No," I said. "But your bank will need help if I decide to withdraw my money. So will your country."

For one brief moment, the two of us sat and looked at each other from opposite sides of the counter. Neither of us found the words to speak. The manager checked behind him for privacy, and leaned forward as if he were about to impart a dreadful secret.

"How much money is involved?" he inquired solemnly. "A fairly large amount I presume?"

"Oh, yes, fairly," I said. "I have just invested one hundred yen."

In an instant, the manager chuckled and whispered something to the assistant manager and the clerk, who laughed too. And then the woman clerk swiveled on her chair and, from behind a cupped hand, said something to a typist. Soon the truth was out, and a great echo of laughter was filling the entire Aoyama branch of Fuji Bank. The young clerk had become panic-stricken when she thought that the moment I had invested my ¥100, I wanted to draw it out.

Since then, I have not dared to venture back to where she works, in case I am recognized, which I surely will be. I now confine all my personal banking to a grubby machine marked with cigarette burns in a box-like cash center near Tamachi Station.

Letter to the PM

DEAR SIR: I AM appealing to you to make urgent changes to Japanese society, even though they may contradict long-held customs or traditions. In the name of these, too many things have been allowed to continue — to the discomfort of all who live and work here. I believe that businesses and landlords are taking shrewd advantage of the gentle nature and gullibility of the Japanese people, knowing that culturally, they are both adverse to complaining and servile to authority, no matter how ineffective this may be. In other words, in the name of tradition, the Japanese are being manipulated — ruthlessly — and I am calling upon you to both recognize it and stop it.

A perfect example of this is the way they are expected to pay key money — *reikin*, or "thank-you money," as they have been taught to call it — those two months' rent that find their way into the landlord's back pocket, never to be returned.

The simple mathematics are brutal. Before moving to a rented home, people must part with a lot of their savings. They must pay the equivalent of one month's rent to the real estate agent as well as the first month's rent on the property, then two months' additional rent as a returnable deposit. Finally, they must pay that other two months' rent we know as key money.

What is this money actually for? Why does a self-respecting landlord have the effrontery to ask for it? Answers to these questions vary dramatically from one realtor to the next. One, for example, said that key money was "a sort of deposit to restore the tatami mats" after the tenant has moved away.

"But what about the two months' deposit?" I asked. "Isn't *that* to pay for damage?"

"No," the agent said. "That's for cleaning if the tenant leaves the place dirty."

Another agent said that "thank-you money" is a remnant of World War II, when the government allowed landlords to ask for two months' extra rent so they could accumulate a cash flow, supposedly to help finance property improvements.

"But the war's been over for nearly 50 years," I said incredulously, "and key money is causing a lot of hardship to a lot of people who don't even remember it!"

"Yes, I think you're right," the agent said. "But nothing will change. Key money is a Japanese custom."

The most frank reply to my question came from a landlord himself. "Key money is a gift," he said unabashedly. "According to Japanese tradition, you *must* give the landlord a present."

"It may well be tradition," I said, "but that doesn't make it right!"

It sure doesn't, Mr. Prime Minister. Not in the 1990s. I happen to be a landlord myself, owning property in Montreal and Miami. In both places, the laws state very clearly what I may charge. Rent in advance in the form of a returnable deposit against damage is legal in Florida but not in Montreal. A quick way to end up in prison in either of these places, however, would be to ask a tenant for a gift of money as a prerequisite to validating the lease. In civilized countries, where key money has long been outlawed, the police call the act of asking for a gift extortion, and sometimes even fraud. Whichever way you look at it, it would certainly be construed as an attempt to obtain money under a false pretense — especially if the landlord wanted his "thank-you" money every two years, which is often the case.

Admittedly, Japan and North America are culturally removed from one another, and cultural differences must always be respected. A perplexity, however, exists in the minds of all good, honest people who seek to stay here: Since Japan has carved an industrial revolution out of copying the very best Britain and America has had to offer, perhaps the time has come for it to emulate the best of Britain's and America's consumer protection laws.

Morally, Mr. Prime Minister, key money is wrong because it is designed to keep landlords wealthy at the expense of those who can ill afford it. As a retired district prosecutor in Nerima-ku says, "Key money is a nasty trick. It is as simple as that." Legally, he agrees that when moving into an apartment actually depends upon whether or not this money is paid, it becomes what all too many Japanese real estate agents find too difficult to say — a *bribe*.

In any civilized culture, paying a bribe — or asking for one — is considered a despicable crime. Why not in Japan, Mr. Prime Minister?

Business at dinner?

LET ME TELL YOU ABOUT another man I've met since arriving in Tokyo — Clive C., of Ohio. He was, and still is, an irrepressible American who tried to penetrate the Japanese market here with an array of well-proven products — like golf clubs, kitchen utensils, cake mixes, beer, furniture, cookies, and designer T-shirts, but who, sweating profusely each day from many hours on foot under a hot Tokyo sun, so often felt like giving up.

But he didn't. In the two years Clive C. has been in Japan, he has called on more than 40 Japanese companies many times over, and finally, following his tenth attempt to sign a contract with one of them, got a call from the vice president — inviting him to dinner at Tokyo's Imperial Hotel.

"This is it," he told his partner, Albert F., jubilantly in a phone call that afternoon. "D'ya hear me? I've finally broken through!"

"Great work," Albert said from his office on Manhattan's 47th Street. "Good American persistence always pays off."

So the dinner date arrived, and Clive donned his best three-piece suit and spent ¥20,000 on a new tie. After all, he was not just meeting the president, but the sales manager, two district managers, the office manager, and a man to whom he was never properly introduced.

Following the handshakes and the first sips of sake, beer, whiskey, or whatever else Clive may have felt like ordering, the food came — and kept coming. "And the laughter and the back-slaps," Clive recalls, "echoed far into the hotel lobby."

In the morning, he faxed the men a thank-you note for giving him such a pleasant evening, then waited for further news from them — an invitation now to sign the "long-promised" contract to buy 7,000 golf putters, 4,000 T-shirts, and 1,000 cake mixes. Let's face it. He'd worked hard enough to get it.

Meanwhile, in his Manhattan office, Albert F. was so nervous about the possibility of the phone ringing when he wasn't there, that he stocked up on two days' worth of food, and stayed there, sleeping on the sofa; in Tokyo, Clive was also afraid he might miss the call, and remained in *his* office without even ordering food. "I didn't want to eat," he says, "in case my mouth was full when the phone finally rang."

Well, it wasn't, because the call never came — not that day, nor the next, nor the next. What the Americans didn't understand was that the Japanese took Clive C. to dinner for reasons other than business. First, they liked him. And who wouldn't? Behind a roguish exterior he is kind and well polished, and always has a joke to share. Second, they felt like drinking with a foreigner because the occasion presented them with a wonderful opportunity to practice their English and tell Americans how much they loved them. Third, they wanted to foster in American minds the view of kind and generous Japanese salarymen who like to drink — quite often to the point of being quite silly — because behind their blue business suits and silver ties, they are regular fellows.

Finally, the Japanese entertained Clive C. so lavishly because they felt that after all the calls he had made on them, and all the pleasant things he'd said to them — like "Howzit goin', you bunch of nice, young fellas!" — they owed him something. What better than a slap-up dinner for six at the Imperial?

In the name of good old Japanese politeness and hospitality, they did for Clive what they thought he would have liked them to do. And, during all the dinner talk, they now said everything they knew he wanted to hear from them: that his golf putters were exquisite, that each of heir mothers couldn't wait to use the sample cake mixes he had left, and that for American products like his, there was *always* plenty of room in the Japanese market place.

Thereby hangs one of the biggest problems a Western business person is likely to experience during a relationship with a Japanese company, no matter how long or short — or intense — that relationship may be. As Clive says, "Cultural differences are very real and can sometimes be a pain in the you-know-what."

His advice: Foreigners seeking to penetrate the Japanese market must understand that nearly all business decisions are made by consensus in a board room, and that to sit at a Japanese meal table does not necessarily represent a passport to Japan's complex and tightly controlled distribution network. An invitation to dinner is usually nothing more than just that — and a chance to have fun on a very generous expense account.

The last I heard of Clive C., he was still pounding

Tokyo's sidewalks with his sample golf putters, cake mixes, and T-shirts. "I will never give up," he had once said.

Damn, damn lies!

CONTRARY TO WHAT was said in a *Japan Times* editorial the other week, it was Samuel Johnson, not Benjamin Franklin, who declared, "There are lies, damned lies, and statistics." That was more than 200 years ago — when the composer George Frederick Handel was churning out his 46 operas and half a dozen oratorios, and shortly after the architect Christopher Wren had seen his brand new St. Paul's Cathedral rise majestically in London's east end. But nothing has changed since. Statistics can *still* be made to lie. They can be made to say exactly what you want them to say, and evidence of this is a pile of figures announced from time to time by the Japanese government — figures that deal with such things as the cost of living, the standard of living, and the quality of life.

The latest statistics tell us that the average savings of a Japanese household are ¥17.59 million. That's about $147,815, which is considerably more than the typical American household could ever hope to accumulate. But the figures are misleading because there are people in Japan who have *untold* wealth, and when their savings are taken into account in surveys of this kind, they inflate.

I base my view on those Japanese people I know, mostly senior salarymen and executives who complain — privately, of course, and never among each other because that's not the Japanese way — that they don't have enough money to fully enjoy their lives. The system, they say, keeps them eternally poor, and most of them have resigned themselves to the fact that they will probably own several cars during their lifetime, but never a house. They can, however, take expensive vacations, if only for five days at a time, with lots of spending money — thanks to generous bonuses.

Enter here more figures. The end-of-year bonus in Japan averaged ¥830,000. That's about $6,000. Maybe the most accurate statistics say that of this, husbands took 12.4 percent (about ¥103,000), giving their wives only 4.8 percent (¥39,640) as pocket money for staying around the house for the last six months in 1989 to look after the children.

Not surprisingly, in male-dominated Japan, 68.3 percent of husbands thought that the year-end bonus had been distributed fairly. So did 78 percent of the wives.

By the way, the *Tokyo Journal* has reported that "the average couple in Japan spent ¥7.55 million on a wedding ceremony in fiscal 1989." Talk about statistics lying or making a publication look stupid! The "average" couple didn't get married in 1989, so how could it spend the money?

What the *Journal* meant, of course, was that couples who married last year spent an average ¥7.55 million on their ceremonies. But even that is wrong. The average couple in Japan doesn't usually pay for its own ceremony. This is usually left to the poor old bride's father. So the *Journal* should have said that the average Japanese wedding cost ¥7.55 million. Since, as we have now been told this amount represents nearly half of the average family's savings — and since I don't believe that the Japanese who you and I both know have that much in the bank — the *Journal* was absolutely right when it said, "Weddings are for the rich."

That's enough statistics. Now for the realities.

Bonuses are part of an age-old Japanese system that is designed to prevent job-hopping — a very subtle piece of what I call "social engineering." Let's not kid ourselves on this point, though. Japanese bonuses are not by any stretch of the imagination gifts, or the proceeds of profit-sharing schemes. Nor are they rewards for work well done. Under the Japanese system, companies merely spread a worker's salary over more than 12 months and, by giving bonuses, are simply paying him or her back what is owed.

If the bonus system were absolutely fair, workers would reserve the right to decide whether they wanted any part of it. They would be able to decide whether their annual salaries should be paid to them in 12 equal monthly payments *without* receiving a bonus, or whether they should take home lower pay each month, but with a twice-yearly bonus with *interest*.

Yes, interest. After all, by agreeing to bonuses — and most workers have no choice in the matter — they are *lending* a portion of their salaries to their companies to invest at a higher rate of interest than that available to ordinary people at the bank. I would like to see statistics that *aren't* lies, and that show just how much money businesses are making by withholding Japanese pay. I guess, though, that neither the companies, nor the government, want to say too much about that.

The salaried worker's discontent

THE SCENE IS A CAVERNOUS office the size of two tennis courts at the Shinjuku branch of the Nippon Telephone and Telegraph Company, and the characters there on this rainy April night, are a cluster of junior executives who have seated themselves around a long table in the corner for their weekly English lesson. There is, of course, nothing unusual about Japanese salarymen and their women counterparts learning English at the end of their workday. Nor is it odd that when the class is over at 8 p.m., half of the dozen students will return to their desks for another hour or so before taking the long train ride home — only to be on duty again early the following day. This, it seems, is how life is supposed to be for salarymen in the Japanese workplace. If it varies from the norm, there is something wrong.

"Once, I arrived twenty minutes late," says a tall, lean man named Tomohiro, "and the boss wanted to see me. When I told him I was tired out, he shook his head and said I had to think of the company and all it was doing for me. I told him I did, and that's why some days I was so tired I could barely stand up. But he didn't seem to care very much." Says another young worker, a 25-year-old woman named Yuriko, "I get home at around ten, go to bed at eleven, get up at five, leave the house at six, and am working at seven. I've been doing this for three years now, and I'll probably go on doing it for the rest of my working life. That's until I get married or find an employer that's less demanding."

Neither is NTT in any way unkind to its employees. On the contrary, it is a good corporation by anyone's reckoning. It has four dorms in Tokyo alone that provide temporary shelter to younger members of the staff while they are in training, a generous pension scheme, a healthcare plan, and it offers two bonuses each year. The trouble is, for men like Hasaki, who is 38, all this extra money must go toward paying off the mortgage on a little house he has bought for his wife and two small children at Kichijoji, on JR's Chuo Line. "If I didn't get a bonus," he says, "I'd be in *real* trouble. Ask my wife."

And statements like this aren't atypical, either.

What *is* unusual about the people sitting bolt upright around the table — the men in crisp, white shirts, their jackets fastened, the women in nicely-cut uniforms — is that they are at last speaking out, openly and with fervor. They are among the growing number of Japanese workers who are beginning to admit that their workplace, as affluent as it is, is a frustrating place, and that, in general, their lives could be better. They are peeling off the lid, so to speak, and such men as Tomohiro, who is 29, university-educated, single, and paying ¥80,000 a month — or 30 percent of his salary — for a room and a cubbyhole of a kitchen nearly two hours from his office, are wondering whether a career with a company like NTT is worth it. Or with any other large Tokyo-based corporation, come to that.

Except for Hasaki, all the men and women who have congregated in that office — some speaking English falteringly while, thanks to world travel, others are proficient in it — confess to earning less than ¥4 million a year, most of which goes on rent, clothes, food and such simple luxuries as going to the movies and drinking. Such forms of escapism make life in big-city Japan more bearable than it otherwise would be. For as another employee, Hideo, who has found a corner in the company's telecommunications branch, says, "What we are all having here at the moment is a life in hell, and with almost no way out."

Is there really a way out? "We hope there is," says Yuriko, who graduated from Sophia University with an honors degree in mathematics but who earns only ¥3 million a year. "We hope there will be a way out. But first we must engage in a fight."

One of these may just have started. Two weeks before, the weekly English lesson had been hurriedly canceled because everyone around that table — all of them members of Japan's largest trade union, Zenkoku Denki Tsushin — had gone on strike. It wasn't what labor analysts would call a furious and prolonged walkout. Nor was it a bitter confrontation. It was merely a Japanese-style, token demonstration that said, in effect, that the workers were fed up with not taking home enough money, and that negotiations for more had been going nowhere. Tomohiro, Yuriko, Hasaki and Hideo wanted a nine percent pay increase but, on the union's advice, voted to settle for six.

"We should have stuck out for more," Hideo says, "but we're only salarymen, and, as such, we don't have any power. With hardly any unemployment in Japan, and new workers graduating from our universities every year, there's always someone else to fill our shoes."

All the people there that night expressed similar concerns: not only about money, long working hours, and the journey to and from work in packed trains, but about working conditions that have been tied for too long to Japanese traditions. All but one of the students said that they disliked their bosses. One man said he *hated* his. All but two conceded that while their superiors — or section heads, as they call them — could sometimes be kind, they were nonetheless incompetent. All but three said they would like to quit NTT, but that the thought of job-hopping frightened them. And all, except Yuriko, who sits at a computer all day long placing customers' orders, and who revels in the opportunity to speak to the public, felt that the company did not have the workers at heart.

"Nor do most other companies that have a monopoly," Hideo quipped. His lips had taken on a bitter line. "Japanese firms have come to believe that when they offer you a job for life, they own your heart, your soul, and your family. It doesn't matter how long it takes you to get home, or come to work. When you sign that contract for employment, you don't belong to yourself or anyone you love any more. You belong to the company, and the boss who watches every move you make!"

"Yes," said Tomohiro. "You sometimes wonder if the boss has been hired specifically to take note of everything you do — when you come in, when you have lunch, and how many times you stop for a coffee or a smoke."

By consensus, those young executives agreed that Japan expects its salarymen, and their women counterparts, to work too much each day and for too many hours, and it is not only making them dull people, but impairing the quality of their lives.

"Overtime is an institution in nearly all Japanese companies," says Hasaki, "even when it's not necessary. Half the companies have got money to throw away."

"Money to burn," says Tomohiro, with a shrug.

"Money to control you with," adds Hideo.

"Well, I can't complain," says Yuriko, "because I've only been working here three years."

Toward the end of the lesson, at around 7:30 p.m., the men and women leave the vast office, which houses the customer service, sales, and accounts departments, and, at the company's invitation, assemble in the fifth-floor cafeteria for an impromptu meal of squid, meatballs, soup, and salad, to be washed down with beer — as much as anyone can drink in the hour or so before the establishment closes. Every Wednesday night, NTT allows those staffers who are working late to drink while actually on duty, an idea not uncommon elsewhere in the Japanese workplace, and one which is said to help keep morale high. On this night, the NTT cafeteria is two-thirds full.

The reason for the reception is two-fold. In the first place, it marks the end of the company's series of weekly English classes. In the second, it is an opportunity to honor and remember a salaryman student — a man of 47 who had been killed a few days before on his way home from work. While riding his bicycle from a railway station near his home in Chiba Prefecture, he was struck by a car driven by a drunken driver. "If the truth is known," said another of the students, "the poor guy was tired and stressed out and didn't see that car coming. We're all tired and stressed out — and we're constantly under pressure to produce. Why do you think salarymen drink like they do?"

Silence falls, and a section boss, a short, pudgy man with flowing white hair and a voice of gravel, rises to wish the English teacher well and propose a toast to the deceased man.

"I know he would want us all to have a party to remember him by," he says, and raises his glass.

As the audience applauds, a student named Shinichi, who had said absolutely nothing in the big office, finally decides to reveal what is on his mind. He seizes upon the chance to make his comments briskly so that the noise — the cries of "Kampai!" and the vigorous clapping of hands, and the cheers and clatter of glasses — will make them inaudible to those superiors seated nearby.

"The reason we work long and late," says Shinichi, addressing the long, cafeteria table, "has nothing to do with our workloads. There often isn't that much work to be done. It has more to do with having to impress the boss."

A colleague seated next to him agrees. So does another the other side of him.

For as long as Shinichi can remember — as could his father, or his father's father — Japan's workplace has been run by older people. Age is such a sacred and honored thing in Japan that it nearly always takes precedence over the dash and enthusiasm of youth, and, very often, youth's superior knowledge, experience, and talent, too.

Throughout Tokyo today, the NTT workers cite by way of example, computer companies are being managed by older men, many of whom have stepped back into the workplace after compulsory retirement from elsewhere, and who know nothing whatsoever about the product their company sells. They are there as watch-dog father figures. But father, say the younger salarymen, does not always know best.

The same is also true at NTT — "and most other large companies like it," Tomohiro is brisk to add. Middle-aged men, and sometimes those who are bordering on elderly, bring middle-aged or elderly ideas into a modern-day workplace. And the brilliant young university graduates who entered the corporation with a mind of specific knowledge, ambition, and an earnest desire to succeed, don't like it one bit.

"So we work long hours to satisfy men like these," says Shinichi, a clerk in the transportation department.

"And if we quit on time, at say, five-ten or five-thirty," adds Tomohiro, "the boss thinks we're not keen, that we're just like all the other employees, and don't deserve a promotion."

"That's absolutely right," Shinichi adds. "Once I left on time two days in a row, and the head of my section called me over to his desk and asked me what I thought I was doing. He said I was jeopardizing my future with the company, and he'd remember it. I think he always will."

Yet promotion is what virtually all Japan's workers

live for — a chance to make more than ¥4 million a year. Their dreams and personal aspirations, after all — mostly to marry, have families, own homes, and afford good holidays — are contingent on their earning power as they approach their 30s and 40s. The road, however, is likely to be tough, unless there are swift, broad changes.

"I'd like to see a political party in power that will stop letting the rich get richer and the middle classes get poorer," says Hasaki. "I'd like to see some of the tax breaks that are given to people who set up businesses also given to people who are going to work in them. And I'd like more interest on my money at the bank — particularly since I've now got this house. I want help with the mortgage so I can spend my bonuses on vacations."

"Me, too," says Yuriko. "I want good vacations. I've never been out of Japan, and people keep telling me I should go."

"You should," says Tomohiro, who spent six months in Los Angeles two years ago, and hopes one day to return there to live permanently. "We should all get out of Japan. At some point in our lives we must see how the rest of the world is living."

Outside the NTT branch office, the rain has stopped. Tomohiro, Yuriko, and Hideo shamble off toward Shinjuku Station, while Shinichi, his black briefcase bulging, walks briskly in the opposite direction. Hideo, however, his tie slightly askew, his brown suit crumpled, talks of having another drink.

"One thing you have to know about Japanese salarymen," he says unabashedly, "is that they like to get a little drunk. That's something else you have to do. Sometimes you even have to pretend you're drunk when you're not, just so you can tell the boss what you *really* think of him — about you being better than he is and not being paid as much! If you're drunk, you can get away with it. If you aren't, watch out. Crazy, isn't it? It's crazy to think that we've got all this wealth in Japan and we can't even make our lives more pleasant. Someone has to answer for it."

Then he departs, too. Tomorrow, as dawn is breaking, the working lives of salaried workers like him and his colleagues will begin all over again.

Unseating chauvinism

THE OTHER EVENING, while traveling the Yamanote Line, I witnessed a disturbing incident. In fact, I was party to it. I rose to give my seat to an elderly woman only to watch — aghast — as a younger man elbowed his way between the other passengers to take it instead. I boiled inside and glowered, the woman said nothing, and the man pretended to be asleep.

Had this sort of thing happened only once, or even twice, I might not have been inspired to write about it. I see it every day, however, and it brings into focus the shoddy way Japanese men treat women, and the way Japanese women have been conditioned to accept it.

Some anecdotes passed onto me may contradict what I am saying — the woman, for instance, who, in the same circumstances, told a man he was rude and inconsiderate, then slapped him across the buttocks with a folded magazine. For the most part, though, such cases of retaliation are rare in Japanese society. Women have come to believe that they are somehow inferior, even when they are on the trains, and this nonsense must stop.

I think I learned to give my seat to older people — particularly women, the infirm, and the handicapped — when I was in primary school in England. Either that, or my father taught me by example. I think, too, that I learned that women were as intelligent as men, worked just as hard — if not harder — and deserved exactly the same rights, from my younger sister. Somewhere, I also learned that they deserved to be respected as human beings. It is so basic, it should not need explanation. Yet I wish I could somehow explain it to some Japanese men.

It may take several generations before the society they control and manipulate finally accepts that women are as capable as they are — that women should be able to compete with men for the top corporate jobs instead of contenting themselves with photocopying, making coffee, and answering the telephone — but until that happens, men can show them some societal considerations.

Most of us know Japanese marriages in which women are simply called "Oi," or "You," and in which the women know nothing else, and we are appalled by it. Similarly, we all know bright, talented women who have been made to feel that the skills they learned, and the knowledge they accrued, are worthless — that top jobs must always go to aged, authoritarian men because that's the way it has always been.

We also know that incidents of sexual harassment on our jam-packed trains nearly always involve salaried men who should know better, and that their victims, the young women they try to fondle, are too frightened to speak out for fear of being ridiculed. It is part of a revolting syndrome that, quite frankly, leaves me speechless.

Why do men treat women like this? It is a simple question and it has a very simple answer, even in Japan. Men treat women badly because they once watched their fathers do it. They act the way they do in Japan — reading sexually insulting comic books in front of schoolgirls on trains, hogging seats, speaking down to women, and overlooking their abilities lest they should be threatened by them — because no one has taught them otherwise.

By far the most disturbing facet in all this is the way these men are impervious to women's feelings. They see no more harm in what they do than the real estate agent who says, "Sorry we don't serve foreigners." They think it is normal, natural, expected of them, and it is about time they didn't.

A lesson may have been learned at Harrods at London's Heathrow Airport — a duty-free shop that is staffed by migrant Japanese who have been hired especially to serve Japanese men when returning after their business trips. Some while ago, the manager was appalled to see the way these men were treating his women employees — and ordered them away. "You can behave obnoxiously like this is your country," he said, "but, I'm afraid, you can't get away with it here. Women don't like it."

The story, reported in the London newspapers, raises the all-important point that if Japan wants to "internationalize," to use that awful word, its men can no longer barrel first into elevators, scurry like children for the vacant seats on a train, and pretend to sleep when a pregnant woman is standing before them. They must polish their behavior — and grow up.

Cup full of luck

IT HAPPENED LATE ONE night when the office was quiet because Big Mike had taken the staff out for a beer. In a flush of inspiration, I was putting the final touches to a column when, suddenly, and against the clicking of my computer keyboard and the glow of the fluorescent lighting that makes everyone around here appear somewhat corpse-like, another colleague, Keisuke Okada, broke the silence. He observed my empty paper coffee cup and declared dryly, "Adrian-san, you've won something."

Me? A winner?

You may have read recently about studies that show that coffee may not contribute to heart disease after all. It is just as well because when under pressure, as I often am, I drink 12 cups of it a day. Sometimes I drink as many as 20, and most of this comes not from the coffee shop, where prices are too high, but from one of a cluster of machines that hogs almost an entire wall on *The Japan Times* building's seventh floor. Statistically then, I was a prime contender for buying "a winning cup."

I had often noticed the slogan printed around the rim — "A cup full of pleasure from Apex warms your heart" — and had been amused by it. But it was a little pink sticker that had caught Keisuke's attention. In fact, he was staring at it intensely. It was intriguing hell out of him.

"Yes," he said, "you've definitely won something." What would it be? I cast my column aside and spent some time wondering.

"Probably a car," Keisuke muttered in a flat, dead voice. He was filling in his expenses and leaning back to admire the little mark he'd made with his hanko.

"A car?" I said quickly. "What the hell would I do with a car in Tokyo?"

"Or it could be key money to an apartment," Keisuke Okada added, rolling his eyes and sighing impatiently. He knows only too well how key money infuriates me, and was egging me on, opening a sore wound, watching my blood pressure rise. "Or maybe it will be a million yen!"

I even spent the rest of that night, and most of the following morning, trying to estimate my luck. After all, apart from a music degree from the University of London and a slew of awards and honors for journalism, no one has ever presented me with anything.

Wait! I tell a terrible lie! I once won a barometer in a knobby knees contest at a resort on the Isle of Wight, off the south coast of England. Then there was the box I received after guessing its correct weight at a garden party some years later. When I opened it, the box was full of women's make-up. Oh, yes, then there was the desk-top calculator I won for being a member of the successful team in a spelling game at a Mitsumine Christmas Party, and the bandanna I won for being victorious in charades at a gathering last Halloween. More recently, my daughter won a bottle of Fine Napoleon cognac at her school's annual fair, but didn't want to drink it — she's only 15 — and gave it to me instead. And a few months back, McDonald's presented me with a pocket radio for buying my 10th hamburger.

Since then? Nothing. And nothing much before. When I was a teenager in England, I faithfully completed the football pools each week, hoping to win thousands. And when I emigrated to Canada in the 1960s, I began buying lottery tickets. When you buy a lottery ticket, though, you merely buy a dream. Mine — this time of millions — never came close to materializing.

I ruefully told some of this to Keisuke Okada, but he was very definitely unmoved, unimpressed. "What does a rich guy like you want with prizes?" he asked. And he stuck his expenses in his desk drawer and lit a cigarette.

"Because," I said, "I like to know that if ever I wish for something, someone will answer me — that if prizes *are* being offered, they are being spread around, and I can be lucky, too."

I am lucky, of course — to be alive, well, and working. But I still like to win when I don't expect it. So the next morning, I retrieved my winning cup from where I had kept it — under lock and key — and, with the help of a translator, went to the fifth floor of *The Japan Times* building to collect what was rightfully mine.

The presentation there took all of 15 seconds. One of the clerks, a callow youth in a shiny gray suit, ushered me toward a steel cupboard, opened it, reached inside, and poked a box at me as if daring me to take it. I did, and opened it hastily. It contained a brown, earthenware coffee cup — a prize designed to encourage me to sample more of Apex's "cups of pleasure"— and I am using it now, as I write this.

Both Big Mike and Keisuke say that statistically, my turn at winning has come and gone, and that when the really *big* prizes are to be won, I will not be smiled upon. In my heart, I know they are only kidding.

Bigotry on Mount Fuji

For those who climb to watch sunrise on Mount Fuji, the event, a great spectacle of nature, should be memorable indeed. In fact, here, in this Land of the Rising Sun, there should be nothing more tranquil. But that is not the way it is. And what has been going on there somehow typifies a lot of what is wrong with Japan.

You may have read how a group of Americans, French, Australians — even a Japanese man and his Spanish wife — spent five hours walking to the top of the mountain. When they got there, they were told by the man in charge of a bungalow-like hut for people wanting to rest there, that this was for Japanese people only. Philippe Fourquet of Paris says that he and his friends were not only denied access to the hut, but, as they sat in front of it to protect themselves from a very cold wind, were pushed away "like animals." Fourquet was kicked while still on the ground.

Another man, Ed Zielinski, who climbed Fuji on a different occasion, said that this same man poked him and his friends with a long pole. "How astonishing to meet discrimination in such a place and in such a time when most nations are fighting it," says Philippe Fourquet. And a Japanese, Keiko Akiyama of Yokohama, says that those foreigners who have encountered bigotry on Mount Fuji should make it known.

Wonderful idea! But make it known to whom?

All this reinforces my view that we treat the Japanese

far better in the West than they treat us here. A generalization? Of course it is. These kinds of assessments usually are. They have to be.

Those Japanese who either travel to the West, or who live there permanently, have better lives than their foreign counterparts here. In the West, they are protected by such public bodies as Canada's Human Rights Commission. There is no such commission in Japan.

When Japanese people want to rent houses or apartments in the West, they are free to do so. Real estate agents never turn them away. Nor do they hand out leaflets in the streets to advertise apartments with the wording, "We do not deal with foreigners." Anyone who said, "Sorry, no Japanese" in the United States, Canada, Britain, France, and most other European countries, would be very heavily fined.

Further, we in the West do not ask prospective Japanese tenants for six months' rent in advance, including a landlord's bribe called key money. Our laws don't permit this — for anyone. And again, there are organizations set up to ensure that foreigners looking for a home are dealt with equitably. In Boston, for example, there is the Fair Housing Commission. And key money there has nothing to do with bribing, or for saying thank you. It is simply what it says it is — two or three dollars to cover the cost of a new key if the original should be lost.

Nor do we turn Japanese people away from our restaurants. This happens to a lot of foreigners in Japan, my wife and I included. I think we are decent people — as are most foreigners in Japan — who do not deserve this kind of treatment.

Nor do Westerners develop such racist appellations as "gaijin" — "outsider with no rights." A Japanese person who is either living or vacationing in any Western country is entitled to full protection of the law, and has recourse in the event of discrimination. But this is not so in Japan. And Japanese citizens who are well respected in the West — and most of them are, by the way — may, after having become nationals, run for office there. Take a look at the names on the Vancouver City Council. Foreigners getting elected to any position in Japan? First they must emigrate. Even those who have married Japanese find this hard. For them, it's less trouble to live out their married lives in the West.

So, the man on Mount Fuji, who turns foreigners away from a hut, and who insults them with racial slurs, must be dealt with. Had I been there, I probably would have grabbed his stick and used it to make his ankles smart. And Keiko Akiyama doubtless would have condoned my deed. "I had never heard of such a crazy man before," she says. "His actions brought shame on us Japanese."

Sadly, the Mount Fuji man is only unique because he wields a pole. Other Japanese people — not all, of course — display their bigotry more subtly by hiding behind antiquated laws, or the lack of any kind of legislation to protect minorities. Ask the Koreans. Ask the Chinese. Ask the Taiwanese. Ask the Filipinos. Ask Ed Zielinski who will never forget his climb to this renowned summit.

"No man like this bigot," he says, "should remain in such a beautiful place."

Death of a briefcase

IT FINALLY HAPPENED, I am very sorry to have to tell you — at precisely 5:27 p.m. on a Friday, as the rush-hour swelled on Tamachi Station, and as the hot sun slid behind the office blocks. I knew it would, and awaited the moment with awful trepidation. Good briefcases are not easy to replace these days. At least, not those with a life of their own and the battle scars to prove it. Mine was well scarred, indeed, and, for several weeks, its handle had been so badly split that I knew the end was nigh.

I never had a name for my briefcase. But if I had, I would have called it something like Albert, Arthur, or Henry because these are names with nobility, if not sonority. They belong, after all, to princes. My briefcase was a prince indeed.

We first met a week or so after I arrived in Japan. The brown briefcase I brought with me was too large to fit into the basket on my bicycle. So, I earnestly sought another, finding it at the Salvation Army Bargain Center at Nakano. It cost me ¥400.

Actually it was originally ¥500, but because it already bore those scars, I was able to beat the seller down. I then discovered that only one of the two locks worked properly, bought it anyway, and took it to Tobu in Ikebukuro, telling the clerks there I was prepared to spend ¥1,000, and no more, for necessary repairs.

They, in turn, assured me that the job could be done for that, or less, and, a week or so later — after having paid only an additional ¥700 — my black, leather briefcase was as good as new.

From that moment on, I grew attached to it, and it instantly became my mobile office. Even so, it was also a sort of shield during mad rush hours, was a potential weapon in time of need, and it adorned the inside of the most salubrious Tokyo offices as I searched for work, even though it had frequently tumbled down station steps. Scars and dents apart, it looked quite impressive when I arrived for job interviews.

A man without a slim, black briefcase in Japan? Well, he doesn't ring true. No one can take him seriously. A professional man in Japan must wear a crisp shirt, a tie, no matter how much breakfast he has spilled down it, have a good watch — and a briefcase that looks as if it has served its time.

Mine was like that, and I now sense exactly what you are thinking. You are asking yourselves what was in it, aren't you? Well, I will tell you. It contained a spare pair of socks, an art collector's magnifying glass, a small screwdriver so I could mend my glasses, a packet of throat lozenges, some old photos of my house back in Canada, some outdated business cards, a pair of scissors, a spare packet of pipe tobacco, an extra pair of glasses, a beard trimmer, a computer diskette that contained pieces of writing such as this one, and a calculator. Somewhere among all of that I kept a toothbrush, a comb, and my resume.

The biggest battle scar of all, I realised as I hurried between appointments, was definitely the handle. Soon, very soon, I thought I would have to lay the briefcase that had seen me through my initial days in Japan to rest in the garbage. I then thought I might donate it as a museum piece, or even raffle it off, but couldn't bear visions of an ensuing rush to buy tickets.

One morning, while cycling to Iogi Station, I spied a hardware store where, for ¥30, I bought a roll of black electrical tape and bound the briefcase handle tightly. It was now as firm as a rock but probably wouldn't stay that way for long, I remembered telling myself. I also wanted to assure the previous owner — whoever or wherever he may be — that what he delivered to the Salvation Army had gone to an honorable and loving second owner. I would always be grateful to him for the way he helped me adjust to a new working life, in Japan. Meanwhile, with a repaired handle, the case would serve to give my possession a new lease on life. Or so I thought. All this was two weeks ago.

Last night, the handle broke again. It snapped while I was hurrying down the main steps at Shinjuku Station, and the briefcase itself fell with enough of a thud to arouse the attention of more than a few commuters whose commiseration I will long remember. Beyond any further surgery, it now sleeps in the garbage at the curbside across the road, and I lament its passing with sadness. Goodbye, dear friend.

Something wrong?

LET'S TALK A LITTLE this week about euphemisms which, as you know, are ways of making unpleasant things sound better than they really are. Euphemistically, people don't die, they "pass away," prisons become "correctional institutions," and instead of using toilets, women powder their noses in "rest rooms." Paid officials are absolute masters of euphemisms. They both invent them and bandy them about, which is why government language or "governmentalese" is uninteresting, senile, and often inaccurate.

Western euphemisms have not escaped the Japanese because they pick up English blindly and apply it to their own needs without question. As you will have noticed, they tend to use a lot of wrong language, and the more you tell them about it, the more they seem to apply it.

Enough about that. I am here today to tell you about the latest bureaucratic euphemisms. These appear in the Tokyo Metropolitan Government's annual report on the counseling center it set up a few years ago to help people who have problems at work. I am amused by the way this official body cloaks the truth in naivety as well.

In case you haven't read this report, I have capsuled it for you. It says, in effect, that of the 30,797 people who contacted government counsellors last year, 373 said they had been sexually harassed. There is nothing amusing about this, of course. Sexual harassment is one of those dastardly sicknesses that pervades every society and workforce, and most of the victims are defenseless women.

But look how the problems are categorized. The report lists 91 instances of what it calls "forced intercourse" and 16 cases of "attempted forced intercourse." I would call these 91 cases of rape and 16 cases of *attempted* rape.

Further, says the report, there were 55 "forced kisses" in Tokyo's workplace last year. I, however, would describe these as 55 sexual assaults by pretty stupid people. After all, who the hell wastes time and energy trying to kiss someone who is quite obviously not going to enjoy it or, at least, reciprocate?

That's not the end of it. There were also 237 cases of "forced sexual contact," the report says. Aren't these really another 237 sexual assaults? And besides the 373 people who said they were in some way harassed at work, another 343 said they had been propositioned, which isn't quite as bad as having to fight someone off, but is annoying nonetheless.

Much more serious is that 72 people told those Tokyo Metropolitan Government counsellors that sexual harassment caused them to quit their jobs, and a further 120 people feared that if their difficulties persisted, they might have to do the same.

All this is not surprising. What *is*, of course, is that nowhere in the report is the word "women" mentioned. No culprits were dismissed, it seems, and no women — even among those who were obliged to find jobs elsewhere — have launched legal proceedings. So the

Tokyo Metropolitan Government not only has a euphemistic problem, but a social one, too.

I thought you'd also be amused this week — or bemused, as I am — to know that Japan has a toothless national Civil Liberties Bureau whose job it is to hear civil rights complaints. The director general of this organization is the justice minister, but, after what he said about America's blacks a few weeks back, I don't know whether he knows very much about this topic at all.

Anyway, the bureau, which was originally established in July 1948 with 150 commissioners, has since grown. It now has 11,640 commissioners — all of them unpaid — who are selected, says the government, by "the mayor or head *man*" of a city, town, or village, for being "of fine character," for having "broad knowledge," and for being "well versed in the conditions of the community and possessing an understanding of human rights."

I find this odd because 3,615 of these people have no occupations, and 2,978 of them work in agriculture, forestry, or fishery.

This is not all that's fishy. Religionists number 1,055, with the remaining commissioners being company executives (751), shopkeepers (638), officers of organizations (436), practicing lawyers (363), accountants (272), educators (244), and others (1,284).

There's just one more thing, by the way: Only 1,754 of Japan's 11,640 civil liberties commissioners — or 15 percent — are women. I have a horrible feeling, and you probably do, too, that something is dreadfully wrong.

Yes, I like Japan

WHENEVER I WRITE A COLUMN that even remotely draws attention to a deficiency in Japanese society, my Japanese friends look at me sideways for a few days, as if deeply wounded, as if I have insulted their grandmothers. They should know that Western journalism is predicated on the very simple assumption that the world isn't fair, never was, and never will be — and that it is the duty of us all to try, as best we can, to see it doesn't worsen.

This job invariably falls to the writer, and he or she does it by keeping politicians honest and exposing corruption and social injustice. If the world were perfect and there was no social injustice, there would be no need for this, and writing — particularly journalism — would exist merely to entertain.

All good writing must entertain, of course. That goes without saying. But it must also inform. To put this another way: The object of writing is to spill facts in an entertaining manner so that they are easy to read and, accordingly, more prone to stick in readers' minds. What *doesn't* stick, is writing that says, in effect, that everything is fine — that things couldn't be better. The quickest way to lose your readers is to tell them just that because, deep in their hearts, they know it not to be true. Thus, I talk about key money, racism, chauvinism, social engineering, political corruption, and the harshness of Japanese life.

When I do, the Japanese must not construe it to mean that I do not like their country. I do like it — very much — but for reasons that may not be readily apparent. I will not fret, for example, if I have drunk my last glass of sake, eaten my last slice of raw fish, or seen my last sumo match. I would, however, fret if the Japanese told me never to come back. While I do not like all that is at the root of Japanese tradition, and how this has been passed down at the expense of the quality of life, I enjoy the ordinary people — the people you and I meet everyday, either at work or on the way to work, or when we are shopping. Without the fear of sounding condescending, I must tell you that I like them very much, and admire what *they* — not the politicians or the civil servants — have done to preserve what I call "the Japanese experience."

I admire Japan's kindness, its on-the-job pride, and the perseverance it has displayed to become a service-oriented nation. I will forever remember the sadness that fills the faces of Japanese people when they cannot provide exactly what you want, in a store, perhaps, or in a restaurant. Nor will I ever forget Japanese humility, gentility, sensitivity, and the uncanny use of silence.

But I will always lament that the Japanese are trapped in a system that stifles their freedom. I shall forever feel sorry that they either don't know this, or, if they do, cannot muster the strength or the incentive or the courage to change it.

I respect the Japanese for their patience, their tolerance of a simplistic lifestyle in the name of tradition, and their ability to be excessively kind — not only to each other, but to people who have known different existences than themselves.

I admire the way Japanese society runs, smoothly like a watch, and how it is geared not so much to the strong, but to the weak. Above all, I cherish Japan's honesty and its freedom from violence.

It would be naive, of course, to suggest that there is no despicable crime here. There is, indeed. But when we consider that Japan's population of 124 million is crammed into only 30 percent of its 380,000-square-kilometer land mass — making it the world's sixth most densely populated country, with about 3,000 people existing in one square-kilometer — there isn't much crime at all. It is encouraging to know that if ever you lose your purse or wallet, the chances of getting it back are staggeringly high. It is also gratifying to know that a woman may walk the streets at night in almost absolute safety in Japan. Unless she is fondled by a pervert on a jam-packed train — and such perverts, remember, exist in *every* society — the worst that can happen to her, or anyone else come to that, is that some night, somewhere on a station platform or in a crowded street, a drunken salaryman will spit or vomit on her shoes.

Saving souls in Shinjuku

ON ONE OF TOKYO'S BLACKEST, gustiest nights, an elderly Roman Catholic priest shambled along a main road in Shinjuku, buttoning his coat against fierce, driving rain, and clutching his big umbrella for dear life. Eventually he struck into a side street in Kabuki-cho, the city's pleasure district, passing massage parlors, strip joints, and sex shops. Finally, in a tall building not a street hustler's cry away from a love hotel opposite the local ward office, he took the elevator to the fourth floor, and entered a bar.

"I sometimes consume too much," says Father Georges Neyrand, a tall, portly 70-year-old with a voice of dark chocolate. But he had not merely gone there to drink. His business is saving souls, and while Shinjuku is his beat, his bar — Epopée — is where he best plies his trade. He opened Epopée 10 years ago to reach many of the students to whom he had once taught *The Bible* back in the 1950s, when they were in their teens. As the 1980s dawned, however, he recognized, shrewdly, that most had since become salarymen, and many of them were lonely and in need of "spiritual strengthening."

But isn't a bar in a gaudy, neon-lit surrounding that is littered with prostitutes and their pimps an unlikely environment for God-talk?

"Not at all," Neyrand says, grinning broadly and clutching a smoldering cigarette in one gnarled hand

and a whiskey on the rocks in the other. "If you try to attract people to Christ in Tokyo into a place where there's no alcohol, no one would turn up. So a bar in an area that's well known and is easy to get to seems proper for me."

He has certainly proved it so. Ever since he opened Epopée's big oak door for the very first time on a hot June night a decade ago, he has baptized 30 people aged between 20 and 70. When he held a mass and threw a party in Shinjuku's Hotel Century Hyatt last Christmas, 335 people turned up. Only 80 of them were Roman Catholics. This Christmas, Neyrand expects 200 people to attend a similar event, and he will be baptizing another three salarymen. His message, he says, is indeed getting through.

Neyrand hails from Lyons, France, where he was ordained in 1950. He had already decided to become a missionary during his studies. But where? "Africa I didn't like," he says, "China was closed, and India was *almost* closed."

His mind was made up for him three days after he left the seminary when three Japanese students who were visiting Lyon, one of them writer Shusaku Endo, asked him where they could find a room and money for food. Neyrand helped them, of course, and then, in 1952, headed for Tokyo where, he says, "the people were eager to explore Christianity."

After three years of intensive Japanese lessons, he spent the next 20 teaching and counseling students at a Roman Catholic center in Shimo-ochiai. But when age began to bear down on him and he felt he could no longer relate to younger people the way he once had, he took time off. He spent three years writing a book on Christianity — in Japanese — translated a novel by Japanese writer Yukio Mishima into French, taught theology and French wherever he could, then pined for something else to do: another way to spread "the word."

Then the idea struck him for a bar. "I have always enjoyed a drink," Neyrand thought. "Why can't my former students drop by and have a drink with me?"

So he began the job of raising enough money for his venture — ¥22 million in all, for rent, furnishings, and a modest stock of liquor. He did it by attracting 89 investors, most of them former *Bible* students, making them shareholders. One of the few who weren't former students was His Grace, the Reverend Seichi Shirayanagi, the Archbishop of Tokyo.

Thanks to the expert help of another shareholder, a publisher named Keisuke Yamauchi, Epopée gained media attention, and lots of it. Reporters and television cameras turned out in droves to interview and film its first barman — Father Georges Neyrand. "Japan," he says with glee, "is one of the few Asian countries that puts no legal restrictions on missionary work."

With this in mind, he rented a small Kabuki-cho apartment just around the corner from a pachinko parlor and a little cinema that specializes in sex films, and learned — as "Georges the barman," as customers called him — how to serve Singapore Slings and bloody marys. Always, though, he had a fine bottle of scotch ready for when the Archbishop dropped in, as he sometimes still does.

From then on, the bar's popularity spread, though it is far from a resounding commercial success. Each night, six nights a week, about 25 customers huddle at the big wooden counter, or seat themselves at a couple of small tables beneath shelves crowded with bottles.

Predictably, most are men who begin trickling in as soon as Shinjuku's big and bustling commercial district grinds to a halt at around seven each night. As they savor their drinks, at an average ¥800 yen a shot, they seem impervious to the neon-lit pleasure garden that sprawls in narrow streets outside, and for this, Georges Neyrand will be eternally thankful.

Two years ago he gave up the job of barman. He discovered that serving drinks from when Epopée opened at 6 p.m., until it closed at midnight, was tiring him. Since then, he has lived at the Archbishop's house and now arrives at Epopée around 8 p.m. five nights a week, just to mingle with his customers and hear what is on their minds.

"On Thursdays I can't make it here," he says, lighting another cigarette and beckoning the present barman to bring him another whiskey, "because I have to give a *Bible* class. My other work must go on, you know."

Once in the bar he confesses to never giving sermons. He reaches the hearts and souls of his white-collar clientele through a quarterly news letter and through simple invitations to them to attend *Bible* classes. There are also gentle, kind words.

"As in all big cities of the world," Neyrand says, "the salaryman spends long hours in the office, long hours drinking with his colleagues, and long hours on the commuter train home. The salaryman is lonely. He does not know his neighbors and usually doesn't see his family as often as he would like. Here he can find friendship away from his work, and the joyous love of God."

In this one small corner of Tokyo alone, there are more than 2,000 bars, some of them the size of half a dozen telephone booths. Probably a dozen — small, dark places like Nice N Easy and U & Me 2 are actually in the same building as Epopée — but Neyrand is unperturbed by the competition. Unlike virtually all other drinking establishments in the area, his does not strive for profits. With this in mind, Neyrand can safely plan another Shinjuku bar, which he hopes to open in April, and is looking for investors. This time he must raise ¥60 million.

"I 'ave to make an apostle," he says, breaking from his eloquent French into a raw and halting English. "I 'ave to teach more Christianity. I am an old man. Time is not on my side."

Maybe not. But Georges Neyrand has already left a legacy — his books, including an autobiography which was published in Japanese in 1987, and a bar he thinks has filled a void. In the first 10 years after World War II, he says, the Roman Catholic Church missed its chance to make big inroads in a country in which only one percent of its people were Christian.

"Because of the war, the Japanese lost their *raison d'être*," he declares in a loud voice, "but we lost our chance. There were not enough Japanese priests and the foreign ones who came here couldn't speak the language. It was a disaster, and the Church is to blame."

By the mid-1950s, and as the Japanese recovered their self-esteem, he adds, converts were harder to come by. Since then, the job of persuading a salaryman that he should go to mass is even more difficult. He has tried to break ground by showing slide shows, organizing Sunday morning discussion groups, and arranging group trips to Japan's hot springs. Nothing has worked better than a chat, a bowl of noodles, and a few drinks.

"With students you can discuss abstract ideas, like liberty and the reason for life," says Father Georges Neyrand. "Not here, though. The approach must be different — more concrete. Our customers like it that way."

Keeping warm

TOKYO'S IRON-FISTED WINTER has closed in. I feel it in my bones. I know quite a lot about intolerable winters, having spent half my life in London where December and January are damp and spiteful indeed. Unless you have central heating in England, it is excruciatingly hard to keep warm there for days on end. Hence, during one sleepless night on a recent visit, I peeled up a floor rug and draped it over my bedding.

For me, Tokyo winters are much the same as England's. The bleak dampness strikes deeply, and it is exceedingly uncomfoftable. Thankfully, my office is like Egypt, even in summer. But my room? That's another matter.

Because, as you know, I refuse to pay key money, I live in a foreigners' house. To the Japanese, my room is an eight-tatami. To an American realtor, however, it would merely be considered a walk-in closet with an unusual straw floor. It would also be eminently unrentable because it has few redeeming features, the least of which is ice-cold running water in a washbasin by the door.

On one of the long walls in my shoe box of a room is a picture window that faces west. From this, on clear days when you can see forever, I can sight Mount Fuji rising majestically into the clouds. Sometimes, though, when a pollution-thick mist descends, the house next door appears to be hiding behind a sheet of wet, gray gauze.

Last winter, my first in Japan, I discovered that when the fierce winds rattled the single pane of frosted glass that separates me from the outside world, the little electric fire the landlord gave me was totally ineffective. Once, after I had woken to find the inside of the window glazed with ice, I asked him if I could install, at my own expense, an oil heater. When he hummed but didn't respond, I interpreted this to mean "no," and reasoned for myself that if he allowed me such a privilege, other tenants would surely want the same, and one of them — though I cannot think who — might knock the heater over and start a raging fire.

Also last winter, I spent a couple of nights in my raincoat. Shortly after that, however, I bought the electric blanket I have already told you about, which was a wonderful investment indeed, and one like it should be the first of any newcomer to Japan. With the gentle heat turned up, I was generally as warm as a pie, except my nose numbed. Then, when I crawled from my futon, I began to shiver uncontrollably only to find my clothes cold and damp.

The problem, of course, is that my window doesn't fit properly, and never will, and that the landlord did not insulate his building. Every 20 minutes, it seems, new houses rise up in my neighborhood, but very few of them would satisfy North America's rigid building codes. Thus, I have had to face the fact that, like most Japanese homes, our foreigners' house, though well planned, is poorly equipped for winter. And my second-floor room, exposed as it is to those cruel winds, is no exception.

Several foreigners I know avoided using an electric fire last winter to save money on their electricity bills. But for me, money for warmth and comfort is money well spent. This is why, at one point around last Christmas, I contemplated moving into a hotel. I even thought of turning up my electric blanket and staying in bed until winter was over. Then a friend suggested that I might do what a lot of Japanese men do during the cold months — spend more time than ever in the office. But that, I think, would have been copping out. Since then, I've decided to meet the biting cold head-on.

A few weeks ago, I began searching the shops for a small convector heater. In the bleakest areas of North America, such devices are known as "garage heaters." They are ugly little black-box contraptions that have each been fitted with a powerful fan that blast hot air into a cold space, warming it in seconds. In Japan, these may not exist, but I sought one, nonetheless, musing on the ironies of a Japanese winter.

For all its wealth, Japan has yet to enter the age of heavy-duty furnaces, water heaters, and sturdy plumbing and — cultural reasons notwithstanding — probably should. Bathing at night to warm the flesh until morning is a fine custom indeed. But it does not help people like me who enjoy spending long hours in a room — reading, working, and thinking of my next tropical vacation. I hate damp winters. I always have.

Bedeviling English

THE NOTICE IN THE GINZA BAR was as explicit as any I've seen in English anywhere in Tokyo, but that doesn't say very much — "Special cocktails for the ladies with nuts." The detour sign in Kyushu, southern Japan, was just as memorable, and maybe quite effective in its way — "Stop: Drive Sideways."

The announcement in a Tokyo boutique could have been taken two ways — "Our nylons cost more than common, but you'll find they are best in the long run."

And the car rental firm brochure could not have put it more poetically if it had tried — "When passenger of foot heave in sight, tootle the horn. Trumpet him melodiously at first, but if he still obstacles, tootle him with vigor."

The best things that can be said about these examples of Japanese English is that they at least say *something*. Others, though, don't. And no matter how hard you try to tell the Japanese that their written English is all too often senseless, the more they persist in using it the way they want to, as though they are trying to formulate a new language all their own, and one that only they will ever understand.

I have seen "famiry" restaurants, the "Bevery Hills Hotel," and a wonderful ad for "Chanpion Sprark Prugs." And who, among those who happened to be in Tokyo in the early 1950s, will ever forget the banner which, ostensibly, wished Douglas MacArthur luck in his bid for the U.S. presidency? It read, "WE PLAY FOR MACARTHUR'S ERECTION."

Totally on principle, I have refused to buy T-shirts emblazoned with all manner of other English written by Japanese — words strung together on the most expensive of garments, no less — which have made absolutely no sense at all: "The sun is tripping merrily round and round, thus have glorious life." Or, "I watch with specific ardor your very sexuality movement and closeness at being."

Really?

With more than 200,000 English-speaking foreigners living in Tokyo at one given time, I am absolutely perplexed as to why they are not consulted from time to time on what, exactly, meaningful written English actually is.

This week, however, I bring comforting news. Japan is not the only country that abuses my precious language. It is happening elsewhere, but with considerably more panache. Thanks largely to the *Far Eastern Economic Revue*, which has collected such linguistic misdemeanors to provide the chuckles — the comic relief, between the straight, hard numbers of international business — I share some examples with you now.

Outside a Hong Kong dress shop: "Ladies have fits upstairs."

In a Bucharest hotel lobby: "The lift is being fixed for the next day. During that time we regret that you will be unbearable."

In a Leipzig elevator: "Do not enter the lift backwards, and only when lit up."

In a Bangkok dry cleaner's: "Drop your trousers here for best results."

In a tailor's shop in Rhodes, Greece: "Order your summer suit. Because is big rush we will execute customers in strict rotation."

An advertisement for donkey rides in Thailand: "Would you like to ride on your own ass?"

In a Vienna hotel: "In case of fire, do your utmost to alarm the head porter."

In a Zurich hotel: "Because of the impropriety of entertaining guests of the opposite sex in the bedroom, it is suggested that the lobby be used for this purpose."

A Hong Kong dentist's ad: "Teeth extracted by the latest Methodists."

Notice in a Tokyo sandwich bar: "Please eat us. We taste of goodness."

So there you have it. Until I started writing this, English was my favorite tongue. I have now come to believe that I may well write it blandly, without character, without personal style — without all the other things that make words sing.

I am heartened, however, by the sign in the entrance of a shop in Majorca. It says: "English well talking. Here speeching American."

Oh, well. Have a glorious life.

Maybe I'll be back

SADLY, THIS IS THE BEGINNING of the end. There have been good times and bad, but the experience has been wonderful indeed. The other day my daughter Nathalie observed, "You have to admit that Japan has taught you a lot." It has indeed, and for this reason, when I finally depart — on March 29 — I will not forget it.

What has it done for me? Well, I was never ever the sole character in this story. There are two others — Nathalie, of course, and my wife Irene, whose idea it was to come here in the first place when she was granted a sabbatical from her job as a school principal in Montreal. She liked Japan so much that her one-year leave became two. Now she, like me, must face life in the West once more, and will do so refreshed, enriched, and invigorated.

One night last November, when it was raining, Irene said to me, "Let's be honest with ourselves. We've not really lived here, have we? We've only ever sort of *existed*." She was right, of course. But that existence, I think, has taught us more about ourselves than anything, and when I reflect on it, I will do so with affection. It has made us somehow content with relatively little — little living space, few chances to socialize, and almost no chances of getting an apartment at a reasonable rent and without all the deposits and key money, which we steadfastly refused to pay.

In this sense, Japan was a challenge. If we were to exist here in harmony, we told ourselves, we would have to make the very best of what we had. Thankfully, money was never a problem, and I can honestly tell you that we came to Japan not to enrich ourselves financially, but to sample a new and strange culture. Somewhere in our psyche we felt we would *unravel* Japan, and get to know how it worked and what motivated its people. For my part, I must tell you that although I have accrued extra knowledge about Japan, I am really no closer to penetrating its strange world than I was when I first arrived here on October 13, 1989.

Japan is a huge mystery, indeed, and will remain one. Perhaps that is why being here has been both frustrating and fascinating, simultaneously. Nonetheless, my family and I have learned a lot from the Japanese. We have been touched by their generosity, hospitality, and honesty.

In many ways, I believe Japan is a truly advanced country, and when we are critical of it, we should always remember that what has proven right for us, is not always the way it should be done for others. We may know, for example, that by our standards, Japan is corrupt in high places. But is it really corrupt when corruption has traditionally been deemed socially acceptable? All foreigners can do to preserve their integrity is to have no part of it.

The lessons we can learn from the Japanese are, I think, how to oil the wheels of social machinery so that they turn, day in and day out, smoothly. We can learn humility and the real meaning of trust. We can also learn a lot about something the West has so blithely swept aside — job creation. Quite frankly, knowing that it was creating jobs for people who needed them most, I would be more than happy to pay an extra dollar for my 99-cent Florida breakfast. Jobs, after all, spell dignity, and that is something the Japanese — the poorest among them — do not lack.

The safety of Japan is glorious beyond words. It has enabled my wife and I to allow our daughter much more independence than she would have been afforded in Montreal, where we live, and at a much earlier age.

More than anything, Japan has brought our family closer together. We always *were* close, but until I arrived here, I lived in a somewhat isolated world of Shakespeare and Gustav Mahler. The acute lack of living space, however, has since made us infinitely more sharing. On quiet nights, when our room has been as dark as a pocket and as cold as Siberia, we have warmed and brightened it — with our daughter's music! I never thought I would share an evening in Tokyo with Madonna, Bruce Willis, or George Michael, but I have counted *that* as a valuable experience, too. A mind, after all, must always be open, which is why I came to Japan in the first place. And a mind must always be fed, which is why I stayed.

I have a feeling — a very strong feeling — that my family and I will one day come back.

Back in time

UNDERSTANDING JAPAN — TRYING to unravel its people, heritage, character, and lifestyle — can be perplexing at best. I knew it would be. So before coming here, I read and read on Japan continuously. And when I arrived, on a sun-drenched Friday in October 1989, I discovered that half the books about it were wrong. The Japanese people were indeed polite, but not always *that* polite, for example, and the food was tasty, but not *that* much so.

The longer I have been here, the more I have become aware of Japan's miracle — not so much in the way it continues to cling to tradition, but how far it has come with all of its cultural and traditional baggage. Few of the books have properly explained this. Yet, it seems, Japan's miracle is so unique, it is this that continues to perplex.

All this was so apparent to me the other day when, with nothing more to do, I visited a museum in which a small Edo period village that once nestled on the banks of the Sumida River had been reproduced in life-size. Stepping into the museum's ante-room I suddenly found myself in a cluster of little stone streets with their stalls, boat house, fire tower, rice store, warehouse, oil wholesaler's shop, vegetable store, and tenement house.

What more could I expect? What the museum had, in fact, reproduced was the tiny neighborhood of Saga-cho, once part of Fukagawa, and what the Japanese call a "common people's" community. It prospered in the middle of last century as a trading center for the million or so people who lived in the city of Edo, which was later to be called Tokyo. There, successful merchants dealt in rice, salt, oil, lumber, and fertilizers, and around them grew a burgeoning culture unique to ordinary people.

About 150 years later, I imagined myself meeting them. At any moment, I thought I would encounter the liquor store apprentice, a waitress at a tea stall, the leader of the fire brigade in his soft leather jacket, and a merchant or two. And strolling those cracking, stone streets, I was watching constantly for the village carpenter, the hairdresser, a candyman, an eel restaurant's delivery man, a traveling ballad singer, a traveling musician, a news vendor, a geisha girl, a sumo wrestler, a street huckster selling sushi, a "monkey show" entertainer, an old woman selling flowers, a few happy children who darted squeaking from narrow alleyways. There was also the chance, I thought, that I might confront the village ruffian and a fortune teller. For such were the people who made the streets and buildings spring to life.

In that museum — appropriately called the Fukagawa Edo Museum, just a 10-minute walk from Morishita Station on the Toei Shinjuku Line — on that rainy, Sunday afternoon, I felt I was actually back in Sagacho, though I had never been there. It had been reproduced — weathered plank for weathered plank, and rusty nail for rusty nail — just as it had been left.

I also caught a lingering smell of old Japan, with its

crowded living conditions and ongoing oppression by political forces, and reveled in the feeling that the people of Saga-cho had possessed the patience and the wisdom to withstand both. In so doing, they let the flowers of urban culture blossom in other Sumida neighborhoods just like theirs.

A lot of the Edo Era still existed well into this century, when Japan so avidly acquired knowledge of the world outside as it sought to make up for the nearly three centuries of almost total seclusion — "like a frog in a well," as the Japanese themselves have since put it.

"The frog at the bottom of the well thinks the well a fine stretch of water," a proverb says, and it speaks eloquently of Saga-cho's heyday and how Japan was content with its isolation.

Another proverb, however, characterizes the *new* Japan, about which "common people's" communities like Saga-cho had no concept — "The frog in the well knows not the great ocean." The Fukagawa Edo Museum is a wonderful reminder of Japan's illustrious past and how, in recent times, it has found the ocean and crossed it a thousand times.

What a week!

I USED TO TELL A STORY about a Christian clergyman who lost his bicycle and who decided to find it by delivering a sermon on *The Ten Commandments* in church that Sunday. If any of his parishioners looked guilty when he got to the section "Thou shalt not steal," he said, he'd automatically know exactly where his big, black bicycle was. When he got to "Thou shalt not commit adultery," however, he remembered exactly where he'd left his bicycle.

I have to tell you that this is not a *true* story. It helps, nonetheless, to illustrate my dilemma. This week was a horrible one for me. On Saturday, I received a letter from my secretary, telling me that the basement of my house in Montreal had been flooded. On Sunday I left my black, ¥600-gloves on the Yamanote Line. On Monday, I bought a Sony CD player and fought my way home with it on packed trains, almost breaking my back. On Tuesday, the CD player went wrong and I had to call the store to ask them to deliver me another one.

That's not all. All week my left leg — the one I injured 35 years ago while playing soccer for the British Army — had begun to give me more trouble than it ever had, "probably because of the cold, wet weather," a friend said. On Wednesday evening, I rushed limping onto the platform at Takadanobaba Station and wedged myself into a jam-packed, Saginomiya-bound train on the Seibu-Shinjuku Line. It was one of those days when you needed a shoehorn to get an extra person into the carriage, and that extra person was me.

On a mad impulse, I decided to be characteristically Japanese and rush from one side of the platform to the other and actually *bulldoze* my way into the carriage, treading on shoes, knocking women over, and generally making a horrible nuisance of myself. The plan misfired, however, because my raincoat became jammed in the door when a railway worker pushed me from behind into the seething mass of people. When I wanted to leave the train at Saginomiya, where I was to have caught a local train a mere two stops to Iogi, I couldn't. I was stuck where I was. The doors on the other side of the carriage opened and not those that gripped my coat. Of course, I could have taken my coat off and abandoned it, but decided not to. Not until I arrived at the next express stop was I finally able to free myself, blue London Fog raincoat and all.

That was not the end of my worries on Wednesday. Big Mike had left early, leaving me with a huge pile of editing to do, and I was thinking about this on the train back a few stops to Iogi. My leg was hurting more than ever because somewhere in the rush, someone had kicked me in the shins. Then, on finally arriving at Iogi Station, I discovered — to my utter horror — that someone had stolen my bicycle. The yellow, rusting umbrella I always jammed behind the saddle had been thrown to the ground, but my big yellow bike, with its black basket and white, plastic bell, had disappeared.

On my stiff, aching left leg, I walked around for some

time looking for it, but to no avail. I was as mad as hell. Since then, though, I have philosophized a little. I never locked my bike because, as they say, this is Japan, and in Japan no one steals. Well, hardly anyone. I had never locked my bicycle, not in the nearly 18 months I had been using it. So, in a positive way, it took me 18 months to get it stolen. In Montreal, it would have taken 20 minutes, if that. "And that's on a good day," Big Mike says.

I am not embittered. I am not even angry. I just want my bicycle back, that's all. I want the thief to know that his work could not have been done at a worse time. I need a bicycle to help me prepare for my departure from Japan on March 29. (I have lots to do.) Time is running out for me; not having a bicycle will add half an hour to my travel time to work.

That's not the worst part. Of far greater worry is this: My bicycle wasn't mine at all. It belonged to my landlord, and he says that if I don't get it back — if the thief doesn't return it, if it doesn't somehow mysteriously end up where I had left it on Wednesday morning when I rushed to work to help launch another *Weekly* — I must pay for it.

No thief would want a stout-hearted, fun-loving, good-looking fellow like me to suffer that. Or would he?

The killing of Carmel Ruane

ON THE WARM NIGHT OF JULY 20, 1989, a tall, lean English teacher named Patrick Ruane was cooking rice in his kitchen, wondering why his sister, Carmel, hadn't contacted him. The last time he heard from her, in fact, was three days before when she took his San Francisco-bound wife, Hanya, and their two-year-old daughter, Michaela, to Narita Airport. Since then, he had gone to Carmel's apartment several times but, on each occasion, she was out.

"I was getting more angry that she hadn't contacted me than I was worried about her," he remembers. "We got on very well, and I loved her very much."

His doubts were soon answered. There was a knock on the door of his apartment in Nakamurabashi, near Nerima, and two police detectives wanted to speak to him. At first, Ruane thought they were on a routine immigration check on a foreigner, or a simple inquiry about an un-registered bicycle. But later, when they began asking him about Carmel and her boyfriend — an Iranian-born vocational school student named Razeghi Mustafa — Patrick Ruane became frenzied. "What's wrong?" he asked. "Is there anything wrong? Is Carmel all right? Where's Carmel?"

"We can't say for sure," the detectives said.

For one brief moment, Ruane, 33, an erudite Irishman, felt there was nothing seriously awry because when the detectives asked for a photograph of his sister, and he handed them one, they looked at each other and smiled. Later that night, however, they took him to Ogikubo Police Station where, in a small mortuary, he saw his sister's body in a glass-paneled casket. It was 9:30 p.m., and his world had suddenly closed in on him.

Carmel Ruane, a slight woman with auburn hair and finely chiseled features, had not telephoned her brother because she had been dead since just after midnight on July 18, 1989, six days after her 29th birthday. She died in the Nishi-Ogikubo apartment of the man who was later charged with killing her — 28-year-old Razeghi. Thus began an investigation of what Patrick Ruane calls "a brutal, senseless murder of a wonderful person," and one which raised questions in his mind about the behavior of both the Japanese news media and a Japanese judiciary system that did not somehow do justice to excellent police work.

The facts of the case are simple. Carmel's death followed an intense, two-hour argument with Razeghi. During this, he was putting pressure on her to marry him. The couple had known each other for about two years, first meeting at a language school, in Shibuya, where they both learned Japanese. But they had immersed themselves in a serious relationship only for about a year. Meanwhile, Carmel had been teaching English in Tokyo, to pay her rent, study advanced Japanese, and attend Tokyo University as a graduate journalism student.

Although a wedding date had been agreed upon — June 22, 1989 — she had not only changed her mind about marrying Razeghi, but, a mere two weeks before, had angered him by making a five-day visit to New York City — to visit a former boyfriend. "My distinct impression," says Patrick Ruane, "is that Carmel had decided that the marriage wasn't going to work, and that she'd changed her mind about it." For all this, Carmel spent a lot of time with Razeghi. She admired his looks and his intelligence, and reveled in his kindness. One day, Razeghi hoped, he and she would settle down together. For the moment, though, he had to content himself with simply being Carmel Ruane's friend.

In one sense, Carmel's murder was like most others. It was domestic in nature — and solved; in another, it took on a bizarre character all its own because of the events that unfolded around it. It was discovered by a neighbor who was passing Razeghi's apartment at about 3:30 p.m. on July 20, when she saw feet sticking through the partially open front door that led directly into the kitchen. The police were called, and, when they arrived 15 minutes later, they found Razeghi lying in the doorway with knife wounds to his neck and arms. Inside the bedroom, they saw Carmel's body, under a futon.

It did not take them long to piece together what had actually happened. In fact, within only hours of visiting the scene, dusting for fingerprints, forensically examining a bread knife found near where Razeghi was lying, and interviewing him while he underwent treatment for superficial wounds, they had the case virtually sewn up. At the height of the argument, Razeghi had strangled Carmel Ruane. Then, to make the crime appear to have been an attack by a third person, he had cut his neck and lain on the floor with the front door ajar, hoping that someone would pass by and discover him.

Several hours passed before anyone did, and during this time — and to make an attack by an outsider seem more and more likely — he bound Carmel's hands and feet, tied a T-shirt around her mouth, and stuffed her body into a suitcase, putting it in his futon closet. As the hours of waiting wore on, however, he removed it and placed it where it was found by the police.

As soon as the investigation had been completed, Patrick Ruane accompanied his sister's body to Ireland for her funeral, but when he returned to Tokyo six weeks later, he discovered two facts that perturbed him. Mustafa Razeghi had not been charged with murder, but with a lesser crime of simply "causing the death of another person," which carries a maximum prison sentence of 15 years. Yet prosecutors were only seeking a *six*-year term. Ruane was also dismayed by several newspaper reports, all of them in some way inaccurate. Worse, many had cast nasty aspersions on his sister's character.

His heart pounding with frustration as he tried to penetrate a language barrier, journalistic apathy, and legal red tape, he began a single-handed campaign to preserve Carmel's good name. First, he objected to a ludicrous report that said the incident may have been a suicide pact — that Carmel had agreed to be murdered if her boyfriend then killed himself. This, of course, was something the police had discounted within hours of finding Carmel's body. "My sister was slain by another person," Ruane said in a letter to *The Japan Times*, "and there is absolutely no evidence whatsoever to suggest that she in any way collaborated in her own death."

Most of all, Ruane was infuriated by a story that appeared in the Japanese-language magazine, *Shukan Shincho*. This contained several inaccuracies, some of them harmless enough, but nonetheless worth clarifying for all those who, Ruane felt, deserved to know about the murder and its background. "Carmel had not been living with me since coming to Japan," he says. "I arrived a year or so before, and she had already been here nearly three years." But some of the factual errors, he maintained, would damage Carmel's reputation as a good person. One said she was found dead in her underwear. She wasn't. According to the police report, she was fully clothed. Nor was she one of "many girlfriends" Razeghi was supposed to have entertained. She and Razeghi had been living together on and off for several months.

The *Shukan Shincho* story also introduced a mysterious Filipino woman and implied a sexual *ménage-à-trois*. Razeghi and the two women, the article said, were often seen walking together. The police knew, of course, that any other woman who looked even remotely like a Filipino, and who visited Razeghi, was, in fact, Patrick Ruane's Mexican-American wife. She often took their daughter to the apartment when Carmel was there, so she could visit her aunt. "All these awful insinuations, which were later dispelled in court," Patrick Ruane says, "tell us a great deal how the Japanese have come to view foreigners."

Having spread so may wrongs through quick and sloppy reporting, none of the newspapers and magazines bothered to cover the trial. Had they done so, they would have got the facts absolutely straight — for the record. Indeed, what would ordinarily have been viewed as just another murder after another domestic dispute, had now evolved into an emotional mess. "I cannot emphasize that there are absolutely no hidden dimensions to this case," Ruane said in his *Japan Times* letter. "My sister was slain because she would not submit herself body and soul, mind and spirit, to the will of another. It is ironic that Carmel, a long-time and ardent advocate of women's rights should have been a victim of the ultimate denial of those rights."

It was partly this that turned his campaign into a blitz of letters — about 1,000 in all — which he mailed to various Tokyo newspapers and magazines that had carried erroneous reports, including *Shukan Shincho*, from which he demanded an apology he never got. He also wrote to organizations he thought might help him. One was *The Japan Times Weekly*. Another was the Irish Embassy. Ruane wanted the embassy to send a letter to all Irish citizens living in Japan, to tell them what had really happened to Carmel. "I am quite certain that there are Irish citizens living here who are not even aware of her death," he wrote. In his reply, however — written on November 7, the day Razeghi went to trial — the Irish ambassador, James A. Sharkey, said he could not accede to Ruane's request because the matter was now before the court.

Ruane waited patiently for the court hearings, hoping they would make the facts of the case better known. They didn't, for he discovered then that under the Japanese legal system, expert testimony is not made public — that it is shared between the counsel for both the prosecution and the defense, and the judge. At this point, he wrote to the Tokyo District Court prosecutor, Hiroaki Sasaki, telling him that Razeghi should not have been charged with a lesser crime than murder, and that he should receive a much stiffer prison sentence than only six years. "I personally lost my best friend and intellectual and spiritual mentor," he said. "I would therefore appeal to you to bring the full rigors of the law to bear on this case... Perhaps if you do so, some other woman's family may be spared the terrible agony that Carmel's family has gone through."

The prosecutor's reply was that the lesser charge would stand — and that he could not pursue a stiffer sentence because legal precedents were against him.

During his trial, which comprised several short hearings spread over five months, Razeghi claimed that he didn't mean to kill Carmel, just teach her a lesson. He said he had bound her and put her in the closet to keep her quiet as the argument reached a feverish pitch. This, he said, contributed to her death by strangulation. The police thought otherwise, countering that Carmel was already dead when she was placed in the suitcase. The worse thing Razeghi did, Ruane says, was to try to make the police believe that the mysterious attacker who supposedly strangled Carmel and slashed him with a knife was a young Japanese man who knew both of them.

To further confuse the police, it was revealed at the trial, Razeghi actually tied his feet with towels and — somehow — bound his own hands. But when he was questioned about this, and other elements of the crime, he suddenly and conveniently forgot all his Japanese language ability and insisted on speaking in Persian, which made detectives' work difficult. One thing he could not beat, however, was the forensic investigation that found his fingerprints on the bread knife he had used to cut his neck. At one point, he changed his entire story and said he had tried to commit suicide out of remorse for what he had done.

The court also listened intently as Patrick Ruane, his voice trembling, spoke on behalf of his family back in Ireland. He told the court that Razeghi had met Carmel, who was one of seven children, about two years before; within a year or so she had begun "an intense relationship of ups and downs" with him. This, he said, was primarily because of philosophical differences about how the relationship should develop. Further, Ruane told Judge Ken Toyoda, Carmel refused to be dominated, and this was in direct contradiction to the cultural view of women that a man like Razeghi held. "He needed to possess and dominate somebody," he said. "But Carmel was not prepared to be that person."

As the trial was ending, and incensed by the way it had gone, the dead woman's father, James Ruane, a race horse trainer, wrote to Sasaki from his home in Tara, County Meath, Ireland. "All the evidence I have received via the Irish Embassy in Tokyo to the Foreign Affairs Office in Dublin," his letter said, "can only point to a callous and brutal murder by the accused who lied throughout the trial and did his utmost to deceive the court in most aspects concerning his foul deed." Carmel's sister, Brigid, a television researcher in Dublin, took a similar stand in a four-page letter she sent to

Ireland's foreign affairs minister, Gerry Collins. She called her sister a "wonderful ambassador to Ireland."

Back in Tokyo, meanwhile, Patrick Ruane was still agonizing. He felt the trial was not addressing all the pertinent facts, and that much of the evidence submitted had been shallow. He wrote to Judge Toyoda to say so. "It is impossible for Carmel's family to come to any acceptance of her death until we have a clear understanding of it," he said.

He claimed that Razeghi had dishonored Carmel and abused her privacy by using, in his defense, a diary he had taken from her apartment without her permission — a diary he had edited by tearing out some of its pages. Ruane also felt it had not been made sufficiently clear in court that Carmel did not have an overwhelming need to marry Razeghi, and that he had known it for some time. And, he added, that there had been very little coverage of what Razeghi did between the time he strangled Carmel to when the police took him to hospital.

So it was, that on March 22, Mustafa Razeghi, his head bowed, was found guilty of "causing the death of another person." Patrick Ruane was not there for the entire hearing because in a fit of rage over the lenient sentence that was about to be levied, he shouted at Judge Toyoda — "I would like to express the outrage of Carmel's family at the leniency with which this brutal crime has been treated here!" — and was escorted from the court.

Summing up, the judge noted that when Carmel visited her former boyfriend between July 5 and 10, it "caused an emotional misunderstanding" between herself and the accused. She had written about her confusion over her relationship with Razeghi in her diary, he went on, and the defendant had, indeed, taken this without her permission. Then, recalling the night of the actual killing, he accepted that Razeghi had been distraught and concluded — astonishingly, in the light of the police department's early findings — that he had tried to commit suicide. Mustafa Razeghi was jailed for five years — instead of six — with hard labor, and his sentence was to include the 150 days he had already spent in custody while awaiting trial.

The case was now closed, but from the Ruane family's point of view, it will never be forgotten. In the homily during the Requiem Mass that was held after Carmel's funeral, Father Brendan Purcell, a professor of philosophy at University College, Dublin, said, "She stands out in my memory like a mountain of truth. I never forgot her crystal honesty, her quest for inner transparency and integrity — something I got to know over lots of cups of coffee either at University College, or in her flat with her friends."

But the greatest tribute of all, perhaps, came from a friend — a woman Carmel had met while living in London 10 years before her death — who wrote a poem in her memory:

If we are to remember her
We must remember her all her days
Not just her last.
A life of giving, caring, trusting
A life lived with open heart
With open door.

Today, nearly a year after his sister's murder, Patrick Ruane is preparing to leave Japan — for good. He is planning to take his wife and daughter home to Dublin, Ireland. "I feel more bitterness because until all this happened I actually liked Mustafa Razeghi," he says. "I feel more bitterness than I would have had the crime been committed by a complete stranger to me. I felt I could trust Razeghi and he let me down in the worst possible way. If he had told the truth and just said, 'I did it, I'm sorry,' I'd be thinking of forgiveness now. But that's not what happened. Throughout the entire court proceedings, Razeghi equivocated, lied, tried to make it sound like an attack one moment and some excuse for an accident at the next, and tried to make out it was all Carmel's fault. Additionally, the mere brutality of what he did will probably never leave me."

Nor will he forget the way the case was handled. "Had reporters gone to the police and reported what they had really said," he maintains, "they would have known the full facts immediately, right from the beginning, and our family wouldn't have suffered. This kind of thing must never happen again."

Akane's new boots

DOUG JANSEN IS ANOTHER of those Tokyo-based foreigners who is a man very much after my own heart. Here in Japan, we share a common dilemma. As hard as we try, we cannot always find clothes to fit us — especially shoes. And prices? To us they are astronomical. That's why, a few weeks ago, Doug's Japanese wife, Akane, ordered a pair of brown soft-leather ankle boots from the American mail order company Eddie Bauer, which is known for providing excellent value for relatively hard-earned money. But, to some extent, her project misfired. And when it did, Doug asked, bemused, "Is Japan *really* serious about opening its markets?"

Akane's new boots were to have cost her $89, with a small extra charge for postage. When they arrived in Japan, however, quite a lot of her hard-earned cash was spent on taxes. Customs officials sent the boots to her at the couple's home in Setagaya — with a bill. "There was a rather large fee to pay for duty on them," recalls husband Doug, a low-key man who has been teaching English at Seisen International School in suburban Tokyo for the past eight years. "I'd say we were both rather staggered."

Faced with the same kind of bill, you would be, too! To calculate the duty Akane owed, customs officials applied a highly complex mathematical formula. Don't worry if you can't quite follow it. I can't either. It would require a doctoral degree in advanced mathematics to fathom it, I think.

The officials:

- Took the retail price of the boots
- Added the shipping charges
- Took 60 percent of the total of these two amounts
- Added it to 60 percent of the original price of the boots
- Took 3 percent of the total of this
- Added it to the total of the above
- Subtracted the original price
- Added that to the original price of the boots
- Handed Akane Jansen the bill

The duty on her boots was a staggering $71.20 — or 80 percent of the price for which she had bought them. That means she ended up paying $160.20 for them, and they are the most expensive things she has ever put on her little feet.

She's lucky, though. Being Japanese, she can fit into Japanese sizes when people like husband Doug — and I — can't. I have spent more time than I care to talk about looking for sweaters, jackets, coats, and shirts with remarkably little success. Collars are invariably too tight, arms too short. Yet, by Western standards, I am an average-sized man who has always been able to dress off the peg, as they say, anywhere.

Doug Jansen, who hails from South Dakota, is the same. He stands 183 cm (six feet) and weighs a mere 72.7kg (160 pounds.) This means that if he were a boxer, he'd be a lanky, long-armed welterweight. But he is probably better suited to basketball or high jumping, which makes his search for clothes more acute than mine.

"There's no use looking all over town for something to fit when you can send away for it," he says. "And anything that *does* fit is probably imported anyway."

Like a lot of Westerners, he has all but given up on expanding his wardrobe here. He waits until he returns to America, and stocks up then.

Shoes, though, Doug agrees, remain a slightly more urgent matter. With all the walking that must be done in Tokyo, they wear out fast. When I enter a shoe shop, the clerks refuse to speak to me. Very often, they pretend not to even see me, and scurry into a back office. They know I am about to ask them for what they don't have — a pair of smart, brown brogues, or a simple dress shoe, to fit an average Western foot: size nine wide, or, as they say in Japan, "a 26.5."

Doug Jansen takes a size 10 narrow, or a 28. Sometimes he has to settle for a 27.5 because the folks in some shoe stores have never even heard of a 28! And if ever they saw one, they'd faint.

Jansen almost did that when he saw the customs bill — ostensibly to protect the Japanese shoe industry.

He shakes his head as he finally fathoms the customs officers' formula. "We are charged duty on both the shoes and the shipping costs," he says, "consumption tax on goods that were not bought in Japan, and on services that were not even rendered in Japan. Finally, we have to pay consumption tax on the duty tax."

And all this money, he adds with irony, is designed to protect an industry that doesn't make nearly enough shoes to fit him.

Home, Sweet Home

NOW THAT I AM LEAVING IT, now that I am preparing to return to the West, you may enter my room. I would have taken you there before, but modesty and privacy prevented me. My room, which a Japanese real estate agent would call an eight-tatami, and which his or her Western counterpart would term a kind of walk-in closet measuring four meters by about 10 meters, has been bedroom, office, and living room for the past 16 months. It has cost me ¥80,000 a month but, with electricity and the rental of a bicycle to get me to and from Iogi Station each day, almost ¥100,000. At least, that's what I have been giving my wife to hand the landlord. And that, I trust, is what he has been getting — money for old rope, I'd say, except I am constantly reminded that by Japanese standards, my room is very well-appointed. It came with a glass coffee table and two bookcases, all occupying the west wall.

My room is a far cry from my house in Montreal or my condominium overlooking the great Intracoastal Waterway in Florida, but it has nonetheless been my home. I bought my heater, as I said I would, so, on spitefully cold nights it can be made quite warm. And I warm it further with great music, principally Rossini overtures, Beethoven symphonies, and a wonderful cassette a friend sent me a few weeks back of the world's three great opera tenors, Luciano Pavarotti, Placido

Domingo, and José Carreras — all singing together in a charity concert in Rome during the 1990 World Cup soccer championship.

If the bookcases, the coffee table, and the little desk I made for my computer were not placed side by side against that one wall, there would be insufficient space for my wife and I to roll down two futon night after night. These run parallel to the outside wall, which is broken by a sliding window. When it is open on summer evenings it lets in a pleasant breeze. In winter, though, it allows cold air to circulate among my clothes, which are strung out on a tubular steel rack near the east wall.

Here, above our heads as we sleep, I have hung my belts, a couple of ties, and a *noren* my wife bought on a weekend excursion to Odawara. On the south wall, between the vestibule, which houses the washbasin and our overcoats, are two large closets jammed with luggage already packed for our return trip to Canada. The ceiling of my room is like most ceilings anywhere. So is the tatami floor, except that on this, I have laid a small rug to take the wear lest I should forget to remove my slippers.

By far the most interesting part of my room is that cluttered west wall. The bookcases are full of files, canned foods, medical and stationery supplies, a little cassette radio I bought for ¥2,000 at a white elephant sale organized by students at the Tokyo Foreign Language College, some old Japanese artifacts, two alarm clocks so we can always have a second opinion on what time it is, a small color television set that cannot pull in stations without an antenna, and a little redwood bookshelf I found in the garbage. This I scrubbed clean and set on the coffee table to house the heater.

Whatever you do, please don't tell my landlord I've been plucking items from the garbage and bringing them into his house, or he'll have a blue fit. The Japanese look upon anything secondhand with disdain. We in the West, however, look upon the garbage as a trove of treasures, and — like those friends who have found radio sets, suitcases, and tables on the heap — pursue it with abandon.

Some of the pictures above the bookcases, the coffee table, and that secondhand radio may interest you, too. My wife took them in Nara, Nikko, Kyoto, Hiroshima, and Miyajima when she broke loose from Tokyo with a JR pass that gave her unlimited travel for one week. They show temples, shrines, mountains, islands, parks, and many new Japanese friends. One of the photographs shows Irene bundled against the wind when she took a boat ride on a distant lake.

There are also pictures of my in-laws, former students, and old friends back in Canada, principally my dentist. But those are partially obliterated by various objects that hang from hooks: my wife's necklaces, a Japanese calendar, and my collection of eight watches, most of which were bought in the night markets of Thailand and Hong Kong.

My room, which has been the center of our life for nearly 18 months, has been good to me. I will be very sorry to leave it.

Nihonjin vocabulary

MY FRIEND DAVID BENJAMIN, whose face kisses mine on the opposite page in *The Japan Times Weekly*, is wrong — again. "When Professor Waller leaves Japan," he wrote a few weeks back, "he will do so with a nine-word Japanese vocabulary." The other day, when we met for coffee, Benjie, as he's known around *The Weekly*, did something I didn't think he ever would. He apologized to me.

"I was only kidding," he said, his bearded face twisting into a grin. "It was all meant in good fun."

"I knew it was," I said. "It had to be."

Then I explained that he was wrong about my language skills — simply by underestimating them. I will be leaving not with a nine-word Japanese vocabulary, but with a nine-*phrase* one. And it's all thanks to my wife, Irene, who had already been in Tokyo three months when I arrived. She presented me with a bicycle, a subway map, and an exercise book in which she had scribbled the first few Japanese words she had learned. "You may need them," she said.

I did, and, in some cases, was able to turn them into phrases. You might be interested to know how I apply my new-found skill:

• *Arigato* (Thank you). I use this when I am in restaurants and have successfully ordered exactly what I want, usually by pointing at a picture. Sometimes, when — to my utter surprise — I am given a full cup of coffee that is *oishii*, I say *domo arigato* (thank you very much). But this does not happen very often.

- *Eki* (Railway station). This was probably the first word I used — "Excuse me, sir, I wonder if you would be kind enough to direct me to Shinjuku *eki*." Eventually, I augmented this word with *doko* (where is) — *doko eki?* One day, a woman I met on a train explained how, like the French, the Japanese speak backwards. Suddenly there was born the very useful phrase *eki doko?*

- *Koban* (Police box). This was especially useful because whenever I met a friend, he — or she — invariably said, turn left by the koban, and keep walking for five minutes . . . Around last Christmas, though, I hopelessly sought to locate the police box inside Shinjuku Station, and approached a man I thought was a mailman. "*Koban doko?*" I inquired in near-perfect Japanese.

"You're standing inside it," he answered in flawless English.

- *Genkidesuka* (Is it fine). This speaks for itself, I think. I am feeling *genki* as I write this, though I don't know about Benjie.

- *Sumimasen* (Excuse me). Understandably, I have used this phrase more than any other, I think. My wife said it was good for attracting attention before asking where the *eki* was, or the menu. I came to use it when bulldozing onto trains. More recently, however, it has been imperative while drawing money from banking machines. Twice last week, I tried to draw out ¥20,000 only to find the machine presented me with ¥200,000! "*Sumimasen*," I said solemnly.

Once, when the machine kept my card, I cried out, "*Sumi* (bleep) *masen!*" and a security guard sprang to my side. "Cardo *doko*?" I said, and he retrieved it for me. My Japanese language skills were definitely paying off for me, if not for anyone else.

• *Ima* (Now). This is also useful. In restaurants I can say to the waitress, "Coffee *ima, sumimasen*." It impresses her. And so it should.

• *Gomi* (Garbage). I learned this when I plucked a bookcase from the curbside. Excessively politely, I recall, the landlord said that the *gomi* was dirty, and anything seen therein should be left where it is. I have since tried to use *gomi* as an adjective: Benjie writes *gomi* columns!

• *Nani* (What). "*Nani ima*?" I asked myself when I knew that I had to return to the West. I'm not sure that it's right, though.

• *Dake* (Only). While packing, I entered a supermarket and pointed at a carton of plum cakes. The sales clerk was all set to sell me all the cakes until I remembered "Boxu *dake*." I wanted the box to house my stereo during the long flight home. I am now also able to say, "Coffee *dake*," and, "*Dake* garbage," but no one congratulates me on these.

Maybe Benjie is right. Ironically, as he points out, back in Canada, or wherever else I end up, I will probably be regarded as a "Japan expert," a man whose two years — and nine-phrase Japanese vocabulary — qualifies him to appear on talk shows, to address gatherings, and to generally spread the word about the real Japan.

So, *sayonara* Benjie! Tell your readers how

"*ohayogozaimasu*" was derived — and passed down — from the time two Japanese men were hunting moose in Ohio at the crack of a glorious dawn.

Created in Japan

BACK IN 1942, JUST a few months after the Japanese had bombed Pearl Harbor to begin the great War in the Pacific, an American writer visited the Tokyo University of Engineering, and was amazed at what he saw. Until then, the Japanese had been content merely to snatch parts of Asia. Now, they viewed the entire world and wanted it — not so much by gaining territory, but by mustering economical strength, too. "This is a *really* curious place," Willard Price wrote of the university. "Believe it or not, it's chief purpose is not so much to teach, but to *invent!* "

In a pool of water in one of the science laboratories, for example, he watched a new buoy being demonstrated. It far surpassed those already in use. Instead of being lit at night by oil or gas, it emitted a light that pierced the fog from neon tubes. How could a neon light be produced far out at sea? By the motion of waves, which generated an electrical current. This, in turn, activated the mercury in the tubes — and there was light, and lots of it!

In other departments, other inventions were being developed. A researcher was working on synthetic rubber. Another was making a paint that did not peel, another cement that would not crack. Yet another scientist was working on an electric organ that could be played without touching it — merely by passing a hand through the air above it.

Then there was a store room rather like a refrigerator, in which the temperature was 40 degrees below zero. An adjacent room was hot and steaming with a humidity of 85 percent and a temperature of 85 degrees. Both were used to test medicines, food, clothing, and building materials for use in the bitterly cold Manchurian winter or the hot tropical summer. And of Japan's sudden foray into technological development and invention, Dr. Hiroshi Kinoshita, then director of research said, as he ushered Price through the university's maze of corridors and its busy laboratories, "We have learned much from the West."

In a dark, mysterious room where nothing to ordinary senses was happening, he added, "There are sounds here. But you can't hear them."

Japanese technology — and the invention behind it — was not only taking root but commanding attention with a vengeance at a time when it needed it most. No other nation, after all, had so avidly acquired so much knowledge of the world in so short a period of time than Japan, as she tried to make herself truly international. At first, though, her pre-war inventions were merely imitations of Western ways, and Westerners were flattered by them. But the Japanese secretly meant business, though many Western industrialists may have been slow to recognize it.

"Most of us believe to this day that the Japanese are incapable of creativity for a variety of social or cultural reasons," says the author of the book *Made in Japan*, an American named Sheridan Tatsuno, "but I don't believe that history is destiny. Frankly, I believe that many Westerners suffer from self-serving pride. They often don't bother to look to Asia for new ideas." And he adds, "The problem is that Americans, for example, always look at their own inventions, then look to see if the Japanese are copying. We usually overlook areas where we are weak — and where the Japanese are the inventors or the creators."

Today, of course, Japan is no longer the frog that is content to remain at the bottom of the well, ignorant of the great ocean beyond. Far from it. She now sees the whole world more clearly than ever, and wants it economically. Hence, once indeed content to merely copy Western ways, she is striking out on her own even more, and this may explain why, last year alone, 20 percent of all U.S. patents were filed by Japanese companies like Mitsubishi and Sony.

Predictably, things were better at home. In recent times, Japanese creations have included such diverse items as bioceramic teeth (false teeth layered with protein over ceramic), such medical electronic equipment as pacemakers, biosensors, and electronic toilets which can perform swift and accurate urinalysis for more than 20 chemicals. Remarkably, these can be linked by telephone lines to hospitals and clinics worldwide, to provide patients with instant monitoring and diagnosis. "The Japanese are prolific inventors indeed," says Tatsuno, who is also president of a California-based company called NeoConcepts, "but the sad truth is that most foreigners are unaware of their ideas."

To some degree this is understandable. One problem is being able to actually identify significant Japanese patents. For one, the Japanese are reputed to patent virtually "everything in sight," Tatsuno adds. For two, almost all are registered in the Japanese language, which few people can read. For three, most inventors copy from each other anyway — right across the world — and in the vast outpouring of products they create, it is difficult to ascertain what belongs to whom. Added to these are those cultural differences and deep historical traits that were deemed to somehow impair Japan's ability to create anything new. The West had always been entertained by the mysterious ways of what it called "the funny little people" who slept on the floor and who ate raw fish, and never took them seriously. To the Westerner, the Japanese always donned their clothes incorrectly, appeared in underwear without bothering about trousers, or affected a frock coat with straw hat and breeches.

The West was also somewhat bemused by the importance Japan placed on tradition, politeness, and first appearances, and these traits were real. In 1853 and 1854, for example, when Commodore Matthew Perry was sent by America to try to encourage Japan to open its doors to outsiders after three centuries of almost total isolation, he dealt with the Shogun. When he addressed this man as the Emperor, no one corrected him. Not only that, an ordinary policeman passed himself off as the vice-governor of Uraga. And at a glittering reception, two petty officials pretended to be princes and pompously received the letter Perry had brought with him from the U.S. president. The regal-looking chair upon which Perry sat during this audience, by the way — a chair that was there to impress him — had been hauled in from a nearby funeral parlor! Not much had changed when, in 1872, Japan's first railway line was opened in 1872 between Shimbashi, Tokyo, and the port of Yokohama. As though somehow unprepared for this new mode of transportation, the Japanese boarded their first train with some interest, but not before leaving their shoes on the platform because they had been taught never to step under a roof with them on. They then promptly broke the carriage windows by thrusting out their heads, not thinking that anything else could possibly cover a window but rice paper. It was soon necessary to paint a white bar across each pane in order to convince them that a transparent substance could, in fact, be hard.

Shortly afterwards, when large stores began appearing, mostly in Ginza and Otemachi, their windows bore big signs: "This is glass."

Toward the end of the 19th century, when communications began, the Japanese actually "watched" the first telegraph wires, trying to "see" messages as they traveled along them. Some of these same people said that the wires must have been hollow. Others were convinced that they moved. Country folk were emphatic that telegraphy was all "Christian deviltry" anyway, and mobs tore down the equipment.

Nonetheless, the first telephones were installed in factories around 1912. Everything was fine until they were accused of spreading cholera from the caller to the listener. And during the Great Kanto Earthquake of 1923, which leveled huge areas of Tokyo and Yokohama, killing more than 100,000 people, a lot of foreigners weren't rescued because, it was believed, the disaster has been caused by those gods who were angered by their presence.

When the Japanese first tried to copy Western machines, they blundered badly. Their first steamers, for instance, toppled over. Or the boilers blew up. Or the captain forgot how to stop his vessel and kept it going until it struck a mudbank. "We got the impression," said Willard Price, "that the Japanese were becoming a reflection, and only a very pale reflection, of ourselves. They were only trailers, followers, stumbling along the path we made. Of course, we would always be ahead of them." Westerners weren't, though. Japan's blunders were short-lived. Modern history has told us that. Consider what happened to Britain's cotton industry. Manufacturers from Manchester, England, then the cotton capital, taught the Japanese how to spin yarn, and sold them looms. That was back in the 1930s. Soon Japan was able to make cotton shirts, send them halfway around the world, and actually sell them in Manchester's stores for less than the shirts that had been made there. That wasn't all. A Japanese man named Toyoda invented a better loom which could do more, but with less attention. In a Manchester mill, a woman could tend eight machines at a time. In a Japanese mill, she could tend as many as 60!

Manchester stubbornly refused to believe what had happened. Not until all world markets were flooded with Japanese cottons at prices from a third to a tenth of those in Manchester, and the cotton capital had moved to Japan, did the men of Manchester bother to find out what had gone wrong. When they did, they dashed off to Japan — to study the cotton industry they had pioneered. This time, they took no looms. Instead, after they had inspected the Japanese mills, they paid

¥1 million for the license rights to use the Toyoda loom back in their home town.

By the time they did so, however, Japanese engineers had begun to make their own loom more efficient. Their success is indicated by this amazing fact: Before World War II stopped trade, Japan could buy the raw cotton in India, pay the freight on it to Japan, process it, pay freight back to India, pay an import duty, and sell goods in India for less than the price of cottons made there. To beat Manchester, where manufacturing costs were high, was one thing. To beat India, where costs were even less than in Japan, was another. And it gave a sober warning to the textile industry worldwide.

Japan was long first in silk, a distinction more recently given over to China and Thailand. At one time, she produced more than 70 percent of the world's supply. This was not because the silkworm would not do its job in any other country or climate, but because Japan had scientifically bred better silkworms, distributed silkworm eggs adapted to each district, and always equipped her mills with the latest machinery. The West, meanwhile, searched for a way to circumvent her and developed "artificial silk," later calling it rayon. Seeing the silk industry threatened, Japan promptly stole a march on Western competitors by becoming her own competitor. She built rayon plants and was soon exporting more rayon than any other country in the world.

The familiar comment then, that the Japanese copy everything and invent nothing, is only half true. The Japanese always have copied everything. But they have invented as well. Back in the 1940s, the Imperial Patent

Bureau employed 800 skilled examiners to handle 100,000 applications that poured in each year. Then, about 20,000 inventions were allowed patents annually, and industrialists in both Europe and America watched Japanese inventions with an astute eye, acquiring many of them for themselves.

A magnetized steel spindle that revolutionized certain electrical instruments the world over was invented by a Japanese. The rights to manufacture this in Germany were bought by the Bosch Magneto Company for $300,000. The inventor of a new electric battery did better, though. He sold the American patent rights for $1 million.

Then there was the typewriter which turned a Western alphabet of 26 letters into words — a miracle unto itself. The Japanese invented a typewriter which, even to this day, carries a combination of keys for thousands of characters.

At an Invention Exposition in Tokyo in 1941, there were other devices exhibited: a talking motion-picture projector for home use, for instance, a home television outfit, a non-dazzling electric light bulb, automobile headlights that could be turned in various directions, a gadget that told whether an egg was bad or not without the need to crack its shell, a building material made of waste rice hulls, and a movie camera capable of making 60,000 exposures a second — fast enough to photograph the movement of sound waves. World War II stimulated invention in Japan like nothing else before it. Lacking metals, the Japanese made radio sets, hinges, and door handles from waste fiber. Lacking felt, they made a substitute out of seaweed and peanut shells. Lacking leather, they processed fish skins and made *them* do. Lacking wool, they made something like it from soybeans. Lacking enough steel to make phonographic needles, they simply made them out of bamboo. Lacking enough rice to make sake, they brewed a sake-like wine from acorns. Lacking iron for bicycles, they made them from fiber or cardboard. Lacking gasoline, they made a combustion engine that ran on charcoal.

One of the most amazing of Japan's creative processes, however, concerned the cultured pearl. This was, in every sense, a real, genuine pearl, and it was planned, not accidental. And because of this planning, its cost was only the merest fraction of what an accidental one would be. Ordinarily, only one oyster in many thousands develops a pearl. It is much easier to find a needle in a haystack than a pearl in an oyster bed. Therefore, when one is found, it is worth a lot of money. But then, if every oyster contained a pearl, the price would drop dramatically.

All this flooded the mind of a young noodle maker named Kokichi Mikimoto who often left his wife in charge of the shop so he could spend hours alone on the seashore. There, he discovered that if a grain of sand entered an oyster's shell, it would annoy the oyster so much that it would proceed to coat the irritating particle with a secretion. When this hardened, it formed a pearl!

If only Mikimoto could put a grain of sand into every shell. Well, he did. At least, as many as he could — then went into business. He went bankrupt three times before he made his process work. When finally it did, his pearls covered the world and he became a millionaire many times over.

More recently, Sony's Walkman and a deluge of other miniaturized electronic equipment like home video cameras and pocket radio sets, have been somewhat overshadowed by inventions on an earth-shattering scale: computerized fish farming, for example. Oita Prefecture's Marinopolis project, in the port town of Saiki, has developed breeding systems that use automatic feeding machines powered by solar panels. The experiments are now over, but fishery cooperatives in Oita are planning to use the new invention very soon.

And Japan, whose silks and rayons are still world famous, is not, by any means, out of the textile business. Three-dimension fabrics, or structural materials made of carbon, aramid, and silicone fibers woven in three directions to create advanced composite fabrics, have been developed by the Research Institute for Polymers and Textiles, a branch of MITI's Agency for Industrial Science & Technology, in Tsukuba. A company called Arisawa Manufacturing received rights to the basic patent in 1984 and began mass-production two years later.

So, since the 16th century, Japan has been in what Sheridan Tatsuno calls "a catch-up mode" and has, therefore, tended to copy Western technologies by rote. But "the pupil always imitates the master exactly in Japan," he adds, "then gradually develops his or her own twist to a skill or art."

Now the urge to create is becoming especially strong, most notably among Japan's leading artists, scientists, and technologists. "I believe that in future," Tatsuno adds, "the Japanese will gradually seek their own cultural roots — ideas, habits, customs, traditions, folk arts, and technologies — and mix them with foreign ideas to develop even more creative new products."

Where will Japanese creativity emerge first? Sheridan Tatsuno submits his bets:

Japanese women entrepreneurs, and housewives who are fed up with the male chauvinism of the corporate and political worlds, he says, will emerge as software programmers, artists, musicians, and fashion designers. They will also enter such fields as interior decoration. Young Japanese dropouts from the system, who reject the salaryman's lifestyle and who want to enjoy life, will enter the video game industry. Nintendo and Sega, and other video game makers, often seek dropouts because they consider them to have more vivid an imagination. Watch out for video game makers to develop stunning two- and three-dimensional animation and simulation software. Aging Japanese, especially housewives and former salarymen who want to do something with their hands, will be looking to market new inventions in a variety of fields.

Those Japanese who have returned from overseas, and who cannot easily re-enter the system, are also likely to develop both new products, and services compatible with new lifestyles. But in general, Sheridan Tatsuno says, we must look to see what the West, particularly the Americans, are *not*. If and when we do, we will see that in all these areas, Japan is very definitely surging ahead.

Funny goings on

IT'S WELL KNOWN THAT humor does not always cross ethnic borders and never has, which explains why more than two-thirds of Britain find Bob Hope boring, and half of America never laughed at Tony Hancock. Some things done in the name of culture, however, can be amusing. I refer to the way foreigners must adapt to elements of Japanese life that aren't quite the same back home.

When I was leaving the house the other day, I suddenly decided I needed to use the toilet. So, I hurriedly removed my shoes and carried them with me upstairs, placing them for a brief moment atop the cistern which, as you know, is the water tank that sends water surging into the toilet bowl.

I'll explain what happened later. For the moment, however, I must share some thoughts. I remembered thinking that small Japanese toilets are certainly no place for men like Luciano Pavarotti. At the beginning of his opera career he weighed 350 pounds, which is about the same as half the sumo wrestlers you see on TV. And what about them? How on earth do they fit onto seats on buses and trains, let alone squeeze themselves into toilet cubicles?

I also remembered a Japanese man who makes a hobby out of his banking. Some while ago, shortly after he had opened a new account with ¥3 million, someone in the bank's customer relations department visited him with a gift. Once, when I opened an account in Halifax, Nova Scotia, I was given an alarm clock. Another bank, in Toronto, gave me a set of bathroom scales. I have also received a barometer, a watch, a calculator, and a box of women's makeup, all for banking.

My most recent gift from a bank, however — for opening an account at Fuji Bank in Aoyama — was a packet of tissue paper, which I could have acquired simply by walking past Shinjuku Station. The last time I had a cold, however, I went there to get some free tissue paper and found no one around to hand it to me.

Anyway, this man who considers banking a hobby, opened his immaculately wrapped gift to discover that it contained soy sauce and noodles, which was fine because he likes soy sauce and noodles. Some while later, and overtaken by the possibility of getting another gift, he put ¥3 million into another bank, and, sure enough, he got another gift — more soy sauce and noodles. Now he has soy sauce and noodles coming out of his ears because he has made a habit of shifting his money every month or so, just for gifts.

When I saw him the other day, I hardly recognized him. He had a bad cold and was wearing one of those white masks, ostensibly to prevent spreading germs. Had he worn a mask in a New York City bank, he probably would have been gunned down by a guard for being a suspected robber. The last time I got bronchitis, I also wore a mask — for one day. That morning on the Yamanote Line I uttered a muffled "Sumimasen," and about 100 commuters scattered like pigeons.

Talking again of shoes, my wife is so used to wearing

slippers these days — and not being driven anywhere — that when a car arrived to take us to Yoyogi Park in Harajuku for her school's annual picnic some while ago, she didn't realize that she still had her slippers on when she met her students. In fact, it was the students who pointed out the omission to her. I can tell you that the slippers did not go too well with her dress.

One of my Japanese students, by the way — who harkens back to when I was teaching English at a Tokyo language school — was so grateful for what I had taught her that on my departure she went out and bought me what she thought was an English thank-you card, which I still keep fondly in my briefcase.

"Congratulations," it said on the front, "on the birth of your baby." But the thought was nonetheless there.

I sure didn't anticipate what would happen when my cassette player went wrong and I took it in to be repaired. To tell me it had been fixed and was ready for me to pick up, the company called me at work one day — at 8:30 p.m. Who is still at work then? The Japanese might be, but not me.

Oh, I almost forgot to tell you. When I flushed the toilet, it set that little spout to work at the top of the cistern. You've probably guessed the rest. I got a shoeful of water and my wife says it serves me right for not adapting, mentally, to the Japanese way of life. Since then, I have been trying harder.

Taking back good gifts

THE PHONE RANG. I picked it up, eager for something interesting to do. Nothing much stirred in the office except the spoon in Big Mike's coffee. It was one of those days when most of the work had been done and I was too mentally exhausted to read, or write, another word anyway.

The caller was my wife, Irene, bless her. "I know what we can take back to Montreal for each of our friends there," she said. "It just ocurred to me."

"What?" I asked.

"A *yukata*."

This business of buying gifts to take back to the West is exhausting me more than writing these days. I thought gift-buying was indigenous to Japan. But it isn't. No one dares arrive back in the West empty-handed after nearly two years in Tokyo.

"Can you take a day off?" Irene asked. "If you can, we can go to Ginza and buy everything together, in one foul swoop."

"If I'm going to take a day off," I told her, "I'll stay home and sleep."

Yet gifts have to be bought, and I've tried to think of everything. Since most of my friends are well-heeled, why buy them anything? They've all got cassette players, miniature radio sets, VCRs, and CD players, anyway. What else do they need? And anyway, as one of them, Vince McCullough, wrote to me recently, "Your return alone will be a wonderful gift for us. There's no need for you to bring us anything."

Vince is the man, by the way, who has been looking after my house in my absence. When the basement was flooded in an unusually heavy rainstorm a few weeks back, he called the local fire brigade to pump out the water. Then he promptly installed a new sump pump. I paid him, of course. But loyal people like him, who can make intelligent decisions on someone else's behalf, do not grow on trees. Of course he deserves a fine gift. But what?

And what about my secretary who typed my magazines articles — about 600 of them, in all — on a manual typewriter, then began word-processing my books when, in the mid-1980s, I installed an IBM computer? And what, too, about my inlaws? And my best friend's wife, Ann, who has picked up my mail, kept me informed of all my other friends, and generally been someone I could call at a moment's notice — "Hey, Annie. Can you send me a nice block of Stilton cheese? I can't find it in Tokyo. And how about mailing me a nice bread pudding?"

Dare I forget her husband, Hershel, the most loyal friend any man could ever hope for? Being a dentist, he has been successful enough over the long years to buy himself virtually anything he's wanted. He's got cameras and stereo equipment coming out of his ears. Maybe I'll buy him a year's supply of socks. Or a sweater or two. Or even a wood-carved Japanese mask for his office. That'll frighten his patients away.

My wife has friends, too, whom I rarely see. But they

are there, and they must be reckoned with. They have sent us newspaper clippings about how badly Canada is doing right now, and reports on mutual acquaintances. Now, anticipating our return, they are making doctors' appointments for us, organizing our cleaning woman, and laying on special celebrations to welcome us home.

They deserve something, too, because as Irene says, "When you are away, you really find out who your real friends are. They don't let distance stand in the way of friendship. They are tenacious."

Tenacious or not, half of them should get alarm clocks. Like most people they never rise to see the best part of the day — the crack of glorious dawn. Hey, what a wonderful idea! An Australian friend in Tokyo tells me that the Japanese have invented a brand new clock that you stop each morning by throwing it at the bedroom wall.

Since most of my friends back home like the occasional quiet drink, I could take them sake sets. But I seem to recall that we took them those when we went to Montreal a year ago. We also gave them dolls, tea sets, chopsticks, woodblock prints, fans, bowls, norens, all manner of battery-powered gadgets, and a lot of other useless things that they have doubtless stashed away in cupboards. One thing more certain, not one of them would look good in a Hard Rock Cafe T-shirt.

So, I'm still thinking. Maybe I should return to the West with an armful of Japanese alarm clocks, or not go there at all.

Comparing life

FORGIVE ME IF I WAX a little autobiographical this week, but it is necessary if I am to make my point — that formal Japan bears remarkable similarities to the formal Britain I remember from the 1940s and 1950s. I speak of those important years when I was growing up. Initially, World War II raged. In fact, I walked to school from our little house in West Wickham, Kent, just five miles from Biggin Hill airport, from which Spitfires leaped into the skies to fight the great Battle of Britain. I knew black nights pierced by searchlights. I still recall the screeching of the bombs and the whining of shrapnel.

Other sounds etched into my youth are fonder ones. Just before he went off to war in Europe with the Royal Artillery, my father built an air raid shelter in the back garden. In today's war, of course, it would be superfluous. But then? It was a comfort indeed, and we shared it with neighbors, most notably Mr. and Mrs. Crathern.

None of the other people on the street ever knew their first names, nor, I think, did my mother. As the shells burst outside, she made them tea.

"Mrs. Crathern, dear," I remember her saying. "Your cup is empty. And what about Mr. Crathern?"

During that war, I spent several months with my paternal grandparents in Paddington, London. My grandmother, a spry little Cockney who darted about in a flurry of apron strings, would invite my mother's parents in for supper — "This is Mr. and Mrs. Barrett," she would say. On all the occasions I saw them together, I never once heard her address them by their first names. Nor the milkman. Nor the plumber. Nor even her next-door neighbors of 25 years.

When I left school at 15 to take my first job, as an office boy for a publishing house, I was exposed to other facets of formal Britain. I was told to wear a suit to work, though a sports jacket was allowed on Saturdays. Yes, I went to the office six days a week — to find that my boss, a sanctimonious man with hawk eyes and a prominent nose, had moored himself at the head of a long table with his staff seated on either side of him. The office was small, reliquary, and nearly always smoke-filled. And Mr. Etherington was invariably first in, and the last to go home.

I have since discovered that the language I used when addressing him was completely different from the language I used when speaking to my friends. It was a sort of English *keigo* (polite language) that could be adjusted according to rank and file — "I beg your pardon, Sir, but I wonder if you would be kind enough to show me the way to London Bridge?"

And yes, Mr. Etherington addressed me as he did everyone else: "I am bound to tell you, Mr. Waller, that you are late — again."

Had I asked directions from my friend Ozzie Osborne, who was an office boy just like me, I probably would have said, "Hey, Oz! How do I get over to London Bridge? Any idea?"

And he would have surely said, "Search me, mate. I've never even been there!"

I met Ozzie, by the way, on a packed train. I traveled the trains, too — for an hour each day — into the heart of busy London, with its cramped offices and businessmen in dark suits and bowler hats.

In my next job, as a copy boy for the *Evening Standard*, the editors called me "Boy." I don't think any of them knew my name. I remembered this the other day when, to my horror, a colleague referred to one of the young men entrusted with menial tasks here at *The Japan Times* as "Boy-san." Mr. Boy? That sounds rather odd, doesn't it — a sort of contradiction in terms. But life in Japan — as it was in Britain in the 1940s and 1950s — is *full* of contradictions.

Unfortunately, my mother died when I was 16. But I still hear her words — "No eating in the street! It's not polite." She should have lived in Japan. She would have felt at home here. And after he had been demobilized from the British Army, my father returned to his job as a senior civil servant and professor at both the University of Nottingham and the London School of Economics, where he rubbed shoulders with great men like Trudeau and Galbraith.

I met these celebrities, too, and when I did so in my father's presence, he called me "My son," and I called him "Sir."

I often wonder what he, and all the other characters in this little story, would have thought had they known that I would one day sample the formalities of Japan in Tokyo.

Sexual harassment: The lid is off

IT WAS ONE OF THE NASTIEST cases of employee abuse Tokyo's legal community had ever heard. The owner of a dress shop faked a theft from his cash register as an excuse to conduct body searches on his women workers, forcing one of them to have sex with him. Later, when the 21-year-old woman refused the advances of her same boss, he harassed her until she had little choice but to quit her job.

A few weeks later, a 50-year-old woman whose affair with her boss had ended, complained that he was repeatedly telling her she was ugly. "I couldn't take it any more," the woman said, "and I started looking to work elsewhere. So far, I've had no luck."

Stories like this typify a trend that is both disturbing yet — in a perverse way — heartening. Until recently, sexual harassment at work was a little-known issue in Japan. Now, though, the lid is off and Japanese women are gingerly knocking on the doors of labor consultants and lawyers to report the humiliation they had been suffering in secret and, in many cases, over several years. "At last," says a Tokyo psychologist, "they're actually talking about what's been happening to them."

The country's very first survey of the problem — conducted by a citizens' group called Sexual Harassment in the Workplace Network — says that the most frequent offenders are married bosses who subtly offer women employees top jobs and extra money in exchange for sexual favors. But when the sex stops, said more than 70 victims the group interviewed, so do chances for promotion.

Quite often, the job ends, too. A 28-year-old computer programmer, who had been sent to her new employer by a staff agency, will attest to that. She was fired because, already tired of her manager's advances in the office, she declined to travel to Los Angeles with him, fearing he would expect her to share the same bed. "Fine," the manager told her. "We'll tell the agency you're unsuitable for the job." Another victim was a 34-year-old transport company clerk who grew tired of hearing the drivers' dirty jokes, and said so. One day, one of the men put his hand down the front of her dress. When she complained about the incident to the company's president, she found him unsupportive. "What do you expect, working with guys all day long?" he said. And to undermine her, he moved her personal locker into the middle of the men's locker room. She, too, lost her job.

Fourteen of the women interviewed by the Network said that men had actually used physical force to gain sexual favors from them. One, a 20-year-old, said she was pushed onto a hotel bed while on an out-of-town assignment with her departmental manager. Several victims claimed they had often been forcibly kissed.

The problem, however, does not rest here. Last October when the Tokyo Bar Association held a one-day phone-in on sexual harassment, six lawyers who took part admitted they were shocked by what they heard. Nearly half of the 138 women who called said that like the young woman in the dress shop, they had been raped at work, or forced to have sex as a condition to either employment or promotion. "And this," says the Tokyo Metropolitan's chief labor consultant, Masaomi Kaneko, "is only the tip of the iceberg."

Typical victims, explains another lawyer, Yoshiharu Morinaga, are divorced women whose bosses take advantage of them knowing that they need their jobs badly to support children. And surprisingly, few work mates ever come to a woman's aid, usually because to become involved might endanger their own jobs. More disturbing is that the occasional liberty taken by a male boss on a female worker has been viewed in Japan for far too long as being as natural as the woman who must serve tea to her superior because, she has been told, it is part of her job.

All this has prompted the Tokyo Bar Association to call on the Diet to make sexual harassment an offense under Japan's Equal Opportunity Law, which was enacted in 1986. Until it is, women must fend for themselves.

So far, only one lawsuit has been filed in Japan. Last November, a district court in Fukuoka, on the southern island of Kyushu, heard a claim by a 32-year-old woman editor who wanted ¥3.7 million in compensation because, she alleged, her boss's persistent advances left her no alternative but to quit the publishing company. She claimed that her problems lasted between August 1985 and May 1988.

Toward the end of her tenure with the company, she complained, the 37-year-old chief editor told others in the office that she was having "physical relationships with clients," and was "promiscuous." When the woman reported these — and other insulting remarks about her private life that the editor is said to have made — the company's vice president told her, "You're a nuisance! Don't come to the office again!"

Social workers and psychologists who have launched an all-out campaign to help women who are abused in the workplace, say that the Japanese media has not been on their side. Some popular magazines, quick to jump on the issue, have coined the words *seku hara*, an abbreviation of the English term "sexual harassment." But while many of them, and several of the larger newspapers, have discussed the issue more seriously than before, they have tended to focus on the sexiness of such male behavior rather than the indignity and hardship it causes female victims.

Some magazines have even questioned whether concerns about sexual harassment will last. The weekly *Shukan Yomiuri* recently published an article which, in a weak attempt to satirize the problem, highlighted harassment by senior women staffers — of their male underlings. The article also attempted to describe what men really think, said a male editor at *Yomiuri*."To me," he went on, "the words 'sexual harassment' are dancing around without reality, and I don't think it's a social issue at all. I wonder how many women are really suffering."

He predicted, "The issue will die within a year," but experts say he could not be more wrong. They acknowledge another serious hurdle, though. The concept of sexual harassment is new in Japan, and there is no consensus — or legal precedent — to properly define it. Says lawyer Kaneko: "Japan lacks a sense of fundamental human rights, a sort of code under which a person can refuse to be hurt in a discriminatory way. But no one here seems to have the simplest common sense to meet the problems of sexual harassment head-on, except the woman who filed the law suit."

Kaneko adds "Men never learn the seriousness of their deeds until they realize that the companies — the people who employ them — are no longer on their side. Maybe, just maybe, the fight for equality in the workplace, and the freedom to be who you are without fear or favor, begins with them."

Meanwhile, the debate goes on. Sociologists contend that the male chauvinist boss has been a fixture of the Japanese workplace for far too long. And, with the surge of women into the work force in recent years — they now number 40 percent of all Japan's workers — there is more likelihood of more on-the-job harassment. There are also more opportunities at the steadily increasing number of company outings and after-work drinking parties where female employees feel social pressures to serve their male colleagues like bar hostesses.

A major part of the problem, says Haruko Sokabe, a woman lawyer who was involved with the Tokyo Bar Association phone-in, is that men dominate the nation's superior jobs, and they "know no other women but their wives and those they meet while drinking." She adds, "Sexual harassment is not a problem of individuals. It's a labor problem, and each company must think about it seriously so that they can make working conditions comfortable for all their women workers."

Some Japanese firms that have subsidiaries in the

United States have run into trouble because many of their male staffers have taken Japanese attitudes to America, which, after years of complaints — even court cases by abused women — has developed stricter practices and laws designed to protect.

Aside from the Tokyo city government, no other official body in Japan either counsels victims or helps settle their disputes. The country's only sexual harassment lawsuit, meanwhile, drags on, and it could be several months, if not years, before it is finally settled. Some support, however, is finally coming from labor unions and women's groups that meet regularly to lend an ear to complaints.

At a recent meeting of one of them, members heard how a Tokyo boss had sexually harassed a woman and accused her of being "disabled" because, at the age of 31, she was still unmarried. The case drew protest from feminist writer Keiko Ochiai who says, "Japanese society may be confused by such a new concept as sexual harassment. But just think about who feels pleasant about being harassed, attacked, or threatened."

No matter who's targeted, sexual harassment is an invasion of basic human rights — especially the right to work under pleasant conditions.

Up in smoke

THIS IS A WONDERFUL STORY about double standards and men discriminating against women — the kind of discrimination, in fact, that somehow mars Japan's progress in the big, real world beyond its ragged shores. A few weeks back, a woman who had been awarded the highest number of points in a beauty contest in the city of Tsuchiura, was demoted to runner-up because, just minutes before the official results were to have been declared, she was seen smoking.

"I got one of my staff to keep an eye on the contestants as they sat in the waiting room," said the chief judge, Yuji Koami, vice president of the Tsuchiura Tourist Association, "in order to be able to judge their attitude."

When the unofficial winner was seen enjoying a quiet puff before facing the audience once more, and hearing the judge's verdict, Koami shook his head and declared, "Her attitude is not good. So I think it would be better to demote her from first place."

Mysteriously, a woman who had previously been placed fourth — not even the one in second place — was suddenly pronounced the new Miss Tsuchiura, which suggests that the idea to remove the unofficial winner may not have had anything to do with her smoking after all.

Let's assume, however, that it did. A member of the

tourism section of the Tsuchiura Chamber of Commerce and Industry apparently asked that the original order of judging be respected, and one of the judges also objected to the result being changed. But Koami's ruling stood because no one bothered to give him a strong enough argument. No one tried to make him understand how unfair he was being.

Now, I don't much care for beauty contests anyway, and I bet you don't either. And smoking, of course, has never been good for anyone. But all this is beside the point. What is relevant is that of the nine judges who sought to find Miss Tsuchiura 1991 — seven men and only two women — six of them smoke. Even Yuji Koami smokes.

Not only that, half the members of the Diet smoke. Two thirds of the executive officers at Sony are smokers. And no salaryman has ever been denied a promotion because he smokes. So why shouldn't Miss Tsuchiura be allowed to enjoy a quiet puff when she wants to — without jeopardizing her ambitions?

Quite obviously it is not as simple as that. "Miss Tsuchiura is an important element in the city's PR," says Koami, "and if she were seen with a cigarette in her mouth it would have a negative effect on the city's image."

That's his argument and he is sticking to it. Mine is that Yuji Koami and his colleagues on that panel of judges have inadvertently shown beauty pageants in their true light, for what they really are. Only a woman's external appearance is taken into account when, in fact, there is usually a lot more to her than how she appears before judges and a drooling audience. And some of the silly questions contestants are asked — "What is your idea of the perfect date?" — and the words they are expected to choose when answering them, do little to reveal anything about how well they can be a beauty queen for a year.

To be fair to the Miss Tsuchiura contest, now in its fourth year, it drew 73 contestants — far more than on each of the previous three occasions — mainly, I suspect, because it did not expect the women to degrade themselves by parading in swim suits. For that, even though they had bowed to the wishes of local feminist groups, organizers like Yuji Koami are to be commended.

But for me, they have undone much of that new-found credibility by making a moral — and shallow — judgment about how the winner should behave. When those 73 contestants were eventually whittled down to the 22 who went into the contest's second round, emphasis should have been placed entirely on how well they communicated with their audience, what they felt about life and ambition, and how well — when they weren't smoking — they might do the job for which they were competing.

But so long as there are men like Yuji Koami around, life will never be that fair. And who said that the poor young woman who was demoted would have been silly enough to have smoked in public anyway? Didn't anyone give her credit for being able to decide for herself when and where it was right for her to light up? I guess not.

Heading back

THIS COLUMN, WRITTEN IN MONTREAL, brings good news for some and bad news for others. I'm returning to Tokyo. People who value critical journalism may exalt in this; those who think that a writer should mind his or her own business may find the idea obnoxious. Anyway, like it or not I'm heading back. And some of my reasons for doing so may be of more than merely passing interest to you.

From the moment I arrived here, late in March, life has been dominated by political problems that are unique to Quebec, and a seemingly ever-increasing dose of crime which is unique to the West in general. One case here featured a retired teacher, known to my wife. He was murdered as he sat in his apartment one night in one of the city's quietest neighborhoods. A former student plunged a bread knife through his heart.

A few days later, the woman who lives next door to us — the 86-year-old mother of the local mayor — lost her jewelry to thieves who entered her open front door while she swept a pathway at the side of her house. Thieves also stole a friend's handbag from the shopping cart she was wheeling through a supermarket. That happened the day before I went for my annual eye examination only to find the area sealed off, and a male corpse lying on the sidewalk.

The man, all of 18, had apparently died during a

daring attempt to rob a bank. He and two armed cohorts entered the attic of the building, spent the night there, and attacked bank employees as they arrived for work in the morning. When the police responded to an alarm, two of the men surrendered. The third, however, refused, electing to exchange gunfire with detectives as he fled. He was felled by a single bullet. I arrived so soon after the incident that I could see the young man's blood still trickling into a drain.

All these events occurred during my first week in Montreal, by which time I felt a need for a vacation in Florida. Everything was fine there. Or should I say, "normal." A couple of young blacks were gunned down in a parking lot the night we arrived — after they had tried to rob a gas station — and a retired engineer was in jail for faking the brain damage he was claiming so he might be able to sue a doctor for malpractice. And there were quite a few rapes and some nasty cases of sexual harassment, too.

Somehow, as my family and I watched this crime being reported on television, we realized we had become somewhat impervious to it. This, after all, was Florida. And in Florida, dishonor has long since been a way of life.

For all this, we enjoyed our stay there, and rented a car so we could drive north for picnics on the beach. Once we got a flat tire, and changed the vehicle for another. On returning it, however, we discovered that the antenna had been stolen. It only cost us $11.50 cents to replace it, but the point was made: that little is sacred on Western streets, and there is no defense at all against senseless indiscriminate theft.

Ten days later, and back in Montreal — once a peaceful city — the crime raged on. A policeman taken hostage by two thugs was beaten up and released. The following day, a man who was on the run from prison, took his girlfriend hostage and, as the police tried to rescue her, put a bullet through her head.

My decision to return to Tokyo — despite having been offered a job as a columnist with Canada's largest newspaper — was made the afternoon my wife visited our daughter's school. On the way she watched with her heart in her mouth as the police dealt with another aborted bank robbery. She heard gunshots and, parking the car for fear of driving into the path of bullets, saw two officers chase three would-be bandits. "I think it's time we got out of this place," she said later. I agreed. We had been in the West exactly one month.

The world is not a fair place, never has been, and never will be. Life in the West has gone wrong for an increasing number of people, and governments are at a loss to know what can be done about it. One day, I know, my family and I will have to contend with this place again. Until we absolutely must, however, we will savor the relative tranquility of another domain — again.

Knowing ourselves

WORDS DO NOT COME EASILY. I cannot describe the emptiness I felt when, late one cold Canadian night last month, I sold my Montreal home. I wanted to sell it, of course. That's why, just a few days before, I had put it on the market — a handsome three-bedroom cottage, complete with garage, two sun decks, a fireplace, large windows and beehive awning above a white front door, all set so majestically in a meadow-like lot bordering the mighty St. Lawrence River, on which great men have sailed.

I wanted to sell my house so that I might eventually live in Japan without the worry of leaving a distant property unattended in times when street crime is rampant. What struck me most, however, as two real estate agents watched me sign my house away, was that I was also signing away roots. And the following day, as I reflected on what I had done, I felt strangely stateless — a man with nowhere to go.

The money I would have in my pocket when the sale was finally complete did not dispel my sadness. Selling a house is a traumatic experience — like a divorce, perhaps, or saying a fond farewell to a long-loved friend. The experience, I think, taught me a lot about a need that is inherent in all of us — the need to have roots, even if we decide, as I have from time to time, to stray from them. We need to know that there will always be a place to which we may return at will. We all need to belong somewhere; we must know who our neighbors will be, and how they expect us to act.

The Japanese — and this may well account for the success of their society — have found answers to all of these questions. They have never doubted their roots, of course, because no one has allowed them to. And they will always know that their neighbors are likely to be people just like themselves — affluent, middle-class, amiable, polite, gift-giving, gentle, and law-abiding.

In what the Japanese have discovered, I believe, lies one of the so-called Western civilization's dilemmas: Not enough people, especially among the problem-burgeoned younger generation, know who they are, where they belong, why they are there, and where they are going. No wonder. Wherever they have turned — in their pursuit of reliable friends in solid neighborhoods, good jobs in suitable professions, or worthwhile endeavors in healthy leisure — they have been sadly disillusioned.

Much of this has been caused by the absence of loyalty among the people they know, the instability of economies, and the lack of equality in the employment system.

With a university education, the West has long held, young people are automatically assured of getting good jobs. In Japan, of course, people are assured of getting safe, life-long jobs whether they are properly educated or not; in the West, the need for a good education, while still very real, actually guarantees nothing — even in the best of times. I've met young men with doctoral degrees who are driving taxi cabs, and disgruntled lawyers who are pumping gasoline. These are the disillusioned —

men, and women, for whom life, and education, promised so much but which gave so little.

In the West, minds are polluted by mediocre television, a lot of poor literature, a lack of personal discipline, and a disturbing nonchalance. It seems that if Westerners are to remain social animals and be acceptable to each other, there will be little escape from any of these things. The results? Forget the outcast professionals like the philosophy doctors and the lawyers. There will continue to be several generations of young people whose ambitions will be thwarted before they have begun. These young Westerners, and there are millions of them today, have searched outwardly for an identity rather than inwardly, seeing other people as walking mirrors of themselves — or, conversely, themselves as walking mirrors of other people. They have created, and worn, their own uniforms at the expense of the individuality Western society boasts, and have become awkwardly rebellious and plainly unproductive.

The West must relearn much about itself, and this might well happen in school. Maybe — and this is merely a simple, humble thought — while explaining how great men plied the St. Lawrence River in rafts, winning mighty battles in the process, Western schools should teach their young about themselves, their roots, and realistic aspirations.

When this has been done, life's perplexities will probably take care of themselves.

Have I come full circle?

I'M WORRIED, BUT THERE is nothing unusual about that. I have always been a worrier. When I was small, I worried that my mother might never return from shopping, nor my father from war. As a schoolboy, I convinced myself I was about to fail my next exam. As a young adult, I worried that I might never earn a living in a job I loved.

Those who view work as something that must always be serious might find my theory — that work should be fun, and the moment it isn't, be abandoned for something that is — somewhat disturbing. I spent more than half my young life worrying about whether or not I would one day combine being serious about something with actually enjoying it.

In this respect, my worries ended when I first started writing for *Reader's Digest*, and when the editors gave me a rent-free office in which to do so. As each day dawned, I couldn't wait to get there. In my blazing enthusiasm to rush off to do hard work I loved, and which was very definitely serious, I once put on my shoes and socks in the street. Those were the days when reaching out as a freelance writer was at last paying dividends for me. Until the *Digest* beckoned me — as well as such other magazines as *Time*, *The Review*, and *Equinox* — I had worried my way through long, impoverished years I would not have wished on anyone.

The effects of this has been lasting. When I bought houses, for instance, I summoned untold energy to contemplate the dreadful possibility that I might never afford the municipal taxes on them, for I have always feared governments, bureaucracy, and debts. On receiving my first credit card I worried that I might use it recklessly. I didn't, of course. I admit, however, to buying clothes I wore only once before giving to charity.

Even sending sweaters and jackets to organizations that serviced the poor was worrisome. I managed to persuade myself that my cast-offs might never be distributed among those who needed them most. I'm sure they were, but that didn't stop me from worrying about it, or other things.

My friends will tell you how, for 20 years, I kept scrupulous records of everything I earned and everything I spent, fearing that I might one day be audited by the income tax department. I never was. Nor did I ever fail exams. Nor, despite once knowing a writer's poverty, was I ever in debt.

In October 1989, when I first began living in Japan, I suddenly found myself with excessive time to reflect on all this, usually on the Yamanote Line. It was enlightening, indeed. Like a lot of people both you and I know, I had spent nearly all my life worrying about things that never happened, and were never likely to. My very existence had been dominated more by emotion than by logic. Then I began to meet a lot of young foreigners who had crammed everything they owned into a backpack they seemed to hump around the world at will. Many of these inveterate globetrotters had no cars, no houses, no businesses, no investments, no serious relationships to worry about, only themselves and their families. By being "free," they worked at jobs they loved, mostly as English teachers, with both clarity of mind and freedom of spirit.

Longing to be like them, I returned to Montreal in March to sell my house and to scale down my business, which harnesses my book royalties and fees for public appearances and lectures, and directs them into a variety of investments. When both tasks were accomplished, I closed bank accounts I had rarely used and, to further lighten my load, sold or gave away furniture and put my collection of art and antiques into storage, as well as my 1985 Honda Civic Wagon.

Happily, I am now corporately-lean and encumbrance-free. Reducing our possessions and simplifying our business is something a lot of us might consider doing now and then, just to make the long road ahead less cumbersome to travel.

But wait! Have I come full circle? I love my work and feel as though someone has finally lifted the big, wet blanket that has weighted me down for many years. But I am worried nonetheless. I am *very* worried that as my life in Japan further unfolds, I might live through days that are incessantly sunny — when there is absolutely nothing to worry about.

That, for my mind's sake, worries me no end.

Here, in time

I'M BACK! AND IT'S MY pleasure to be chatting with you once more — on the same side of the world as you are. I dashed out of a Doutor coffee shop in Tamachi to write this, on my first day back at work. I rose at 5 a.m. in my lkebukuro hotel room — weighed down by jet lag — arrived in Tamachi an hour or so later, walked the streets until the coffee shop opened at 7:30 a.m., and waited for Big Mike to arrive at the office. I hadn't seen him since he bought me a farewell beer on the wet night of March 27, when I thought, as I think he did, that I was leaving Japan for good.

I knew nothing between us would be any different than it had been because we'd spoken a few times by phone. In fact, I was just as sure that Mike would shake my hand and damn-near break it, as he had when we'd said farewell; for both of us, time would have stood as still as a dew-coated spider's web.

Time has a habit of not moving and I thought about it as I sat at the Tamachi coffee shop window listening to glorious songs by Franz Schubert on my little cassette player, and watching the world amble by below on a new, bright day. A little part of that world consisted of people I'd seen or known at *The Japan Times* before returning to the West. There they were once more, unchanged and traveling the street, as they always had, trying not to be late.

For me, time always seems to have stood still, and this brings me back to my life. Every workday morning in England, I rose at seven, then rushed for a bus that would take me to a London-bound train. For many years in Canada, my working ritual was to rise at 6 a.m., rewrite what I'd written the day before, then escape my office by going to the local shopping mall. Perched on a stool at a fastfood counter there, I savored a black coffee and a bran muffin while watching a different world go by.

Essentially, I put my thoughts — and sometimes my life — in order in that mall, and planned the rest of my day. It was a morning event that had continued with such regularity and punctuality that the women who served me automatically put a black coffee and a muffin on the counter the moment they saw me approaching.

I returned to this fast-food counter after having been absent from Canada for nearly two years. It was one of the first things I did, for I've always been attached to places, no matter how mundane they may be. The staff, I recall now, was, for the most part, unchanged except that one of the women was pregnant and another had dramatically altered her hair style. Yet another woman was grayer at the temples, and, doubtless, so was I. Nonetheless — and notwithstanding that for some people, two years can be an eternity — no sooner had I seated myself at the counter once more than a black coffee and a muffin was being placed before me. Not a word was spoken. To the woman who served me, it seemed, I had never been away.

Such was also the case in the Tamachi coffee shop, where I habitually consumed my morning "fix" and frequently lunched on a *biggu doggu* (Big Dog.) The staff welcomed me as it always had, in a chorus of salutations, smiles, and nods. I smiled and nodded back. Then a nubile young woman handed me what I had needed to ask for only once, yet had always got — a *burendo rahji* (a large cup of blended coffee), topped with a dash of hot water to ensure that the liquid actually filled the cup. Again, to a different set of people, I had never been away.

Big Mike was earlier than expected that morning. He strutted sprightly into the office shortly after nine in a smart brown sports jacket. Predictably, he crushed my hand.

"It's good to see you again, buddy," he said. "It really is."

It was Monday, sunny, and humid, and I soon felt that familiar tension, mounting as it does to herald another deadline. That was when I began to write this. I had to, and quickly. I had something to tell you, and I didn't want to forget it.

Nothing has changed about being back in Japan. Nor has much changed at *The Japan Times Weekly*. Mike is looking smarter and has lost a little weight, and the desks seemed to be piled higher than they ever were with newspapers and magazines. But I am delighted to be in my old seat once more, the one I lent to my friend Benjie. It seems that I have worked here — and known you — forever.

Who lost my luggage?

Do you remember my telling you how American Airlines was supposed to have transferred my blue Samsonite suitcase onto my Japan Airlines flight from Chicago to Narita, but didn't? Well, it finally arrived after having traveled to some far off place where it spent the best part of a day on a luggage carousel: unclaimed, unwanted, and, for the most part, unnoticed.

A note inside it, next to my shaving kit, said, "Dear Mrs. Adrian Waller. We indeed would like to thank you for the patience you showed during the search of your baggage misplaced on your last trip."

It wasn't a search *of* my suitcase, of course, but one *for* it. And I was definitely not patient at all! After two days, when American Airlines didn't respond to messages I left, I called everyone I could think of who could possibly have a solution: people at JAL, who said they were doing what they could, those at the American Airlines' ticket outlet, my Roman Catholic priest friend, who laughed because he doesn't own Samsonite luggage, and an acquaintance who reiterated what I already knew — "People who lose luggage almost always get it back. It could take days. It might even take weeks. But it *does* turn up. You know that."

So I did. Mine was always being lost. Once — and God strike me dead if I tell a lie — it happened when I went to England for two weeks. Thirteen days later, just as I was preparing to fly home, British Airways phoned. My brown leather suitcase, it announced with enthusiasm, had been found in Lisbon. Now my blue Samsonite had gone astray.

The JAL note inside it went on, "Please accept our sincere apologies for the inconvenience you have encountered due to this mishandling. You may be assured that we shall do our utmost in order to avoid a recurrence of the same trouble in future." But that, says my friend, is what airlines always say. Once, when his luggage was mis-directed, JAL asked him to complete a claim form, and promised to send him $200 as compensation. The only trouble was, his suitcase alone was worth that — as was mine, which was bulging with clothes valued at another $1,500. The friend was on the point of signing the form anyway when he received a call from the airline to say the baggage had been found — in Tucson, Arizona. "I nearly got both the compensation *and* the baggage," he says. "That would have served them right."

After four days of trying to explain my dilemma to two airlines, I gave up on both of them. And one hot night, my little family sat in our hotel room speculating what we might do if our suitcase was never found, and how much the contents were *really* worth. Estimates ranged from $750 to $1,600, until our daughter, Nathalie, said it was all academic anyway. The suitcase mostly contained every bit of her winter clothing which, in Tokyo, was virtually irreplaceable. Whenever she tries on a coat, the sleeves stop at mid-arm.

At this point, I contemplated calling Prime Minister Kaifu. I felt — as did my wife — that no one particularly cared about our missing luggage, and that somehow Mr. Kaifu might *make* them. In the process, my blue Samsonite might become what newspaper reporters call "a political football," or "a political hot potato," or "a diplomatic incident."

There was nothing more to do, however, except wait. American Airlines eventually said they'd call me every day with a progress report; JAL baggage handlers told me they were so very, very, *very* sorry about the loss that words defied them. One evening, however, and while my mouth was full of bread and cheese, I answered the telephone.

"We have found your luggage," said a woman at the JAL Baggage Tracing Center.

"Marvelous! Fantastic!" I said. "Where is it?"

"In Mexico."

So here the story ends. Or does it?

The luggage finally arrived, as I told you it had, two days later. Everything about it was fine except that some conscientious JAL manager had done what I never did. He'd inserted his company's note — then snapped the padlock closed, leaving me, having lost the key, to prize it open!

"We hope that we have not completely marred your favorable impression of Japan Airlines," that note concluded, "and that you will give us another opportunity to welcome you aboard our flights."

I will, of course. I never received such friendly words like those from British Airways, or Delta, or Eastern, or Air India, or all the other airlines that have misplaced my baggage over the years. And anyway, who said it was JAL's fault our blue Samsonite ended up in Mexico?

Where we live

IF YOU CALL US AT OUR OLD TELEPHONE number, you won't find us in. We've moved. My wife, daughter, and I left the foreigners' house in Iogi in March when we returned to Montreal to sell our house. Then, on our return, we decided to do what we should have done the last time we were here — rent an apartment.

So, a few weeks back, I signed a lease to rent one — without even seeing it!

Actually, I didn't have to. I trust my wife's judgment. While I was at work, she was being shepherded from one apartment to another by agents working for three companies that have made helping foreigners find accommodation a specialty. Indeed, I learned that thanks to them, finding somewhere to live in Tokyo need not be as painful as many foreigners like us tend to think it is. Each agent showed us at least two suitable places. An organization called Tokyo House Bureau finally found what we were *really* looking for — in Yokohama, and after only 10 days.

It was just as well. During this time, we had been living out of two suitcases in two rooms at the Kimi Ryokan in Ikebukuro where, to get good sleep during the stifling Tokyo summers, guests must plug a steady stream of ¥100 coins into an air-conditioning unit that sits on the floor in a cupboard. Thanks to my friend the Roman Catholic priest, the remainder of our luggage

— another eight suitcases in all, some of them far too heavy for most people to lift — was stored in the library of a monastery in Shin-Okubo. Ten days of a life like this was enough for me.

Organizing the actual move was a project in itself. Of immediate concern was how we would transport our suitcases — as well as the seemingly endless stream of hand luggage that grew bigger by the day because my wife had already begun to buy kitchen utensils. A Japanese friend with a car helped us solve that one. I then spent the best part of a Saturday, and half of a Monday, trying to locate a company called ABC which, I had been told, would transport the baggage from Shin-Okubo.

It wasn't that simple. ABC said they never provided such a service, and I continued to wonder which company did.

Yet another friend, Rick Kennedy, then came to the rescue. Only when he found ABC's correct telephone number did it transpire that the firm was completely unrelated to ABC, which carries suitcases to Narita Airport, and the company I had been both faxing and telephoning.

The energy spent on finding ABC dimmed both my enthusiasm for moving and my curiosity about where we were to live. I had rarely stopped to wonder what the apartment actually looked like. I knew one thing, though: I never wanted to set foot inside a foreigners' house again. The one in which we had spent our first two years in Japan was clean and well run, of course, but offered little privacy. I don't ever want to see a communal kitchen, lounge, or bathroom again!

The day of the move finally arrived. It was hot, damp, and heavy, and, as I suspected, we had collected so much hand luggage that, when jammed into the car, it left space for only one passenger — our daughter. My wife, meanwhile, escorted me to the new home she had found for us, by train.

Given the Tokyo house market, I was very surprised with what she had found: a huge, completely furnished and carpeted Western-style apartment — a condominium, actually — owned by a Japanese diplomat on assignment in France. It has three bedrooms, a storage room, a large living room, and an exquisite kitchen complete with electric oven, microwave oven, and refrigerator. Quite frankly, few Japanese could ever aspire to own a place like this. In terms of both size and quality, it rates alongside anything you would expect to rent in the West.

When we decided to sign a lease, Irene remembered that the apartment also had air-conditioning, central heating, a king-size bed, a balcony at each end, and satellite TV, and said, "I never thought I would live in comfort in Japan! God has smiled on us."

Actually, we could have signed a lease a few days before on a brand new duplex. But when we began our search we promised ourselves not to pay key money. To our utter surprise we eventually came upon a slew of landlords who never bothered to ask for it! Nothing made me happier. My thoughts on paying key money — let alone making it part of a rental contract — are well known indeed.

Salt of the earth

ON A WALL NEAR THE TICKET wicket of Kinshicho Station in Sumida-ku, there is a yellow box. On it, in Japanese, is written, "If you are down on your luck, please use the money in here." And many people have — from small boys who have lost their train fare home to streetwalkers in dire need of a hot cup of tea.

So spare a quiet thought this week for the man who put the box there in the first place — after having launched a charitable organization second to none, and one that has now fallen on hard times.

That man was Eguchi Shinichi, a poet and novelist, who, depressed by the incredible poverty he witnessed in postwar Japan, spent most of the years thereafter helping the victims fight it. In 1956, after having seen one of his friends forced to "sell" his daughter to help feed his starving family of six, he was moved to launch his Salt of the Earth Movement. He personally set up what were called Salt of the Earth boxes, and tried hard to let the public know they were there.

At first, many people scoffed at his idea and said that the publicity he sought was not for the poor, but for himself. Eguchi, however, was undaunted. So were the estimated 100,000 followers he had recruited. He continued his publicity campaign anyway, and little yellow boxes, each containing a few hundred yen, began springing up everywhere.

On the top of the one in Kinshicho Station is written, "Salt of the Earth Box No. 731." At the movement's prime, in the mid-1960s, there were 732 of them sprinkled the length and breadth of Japan, with a further nine in the United States and one in Vancouver, Canada. Eguchi Shinichi's little dream had gained a lot of steam.

Benevolent passersby eagerly dropped coins in the boxes to keep them going, and they were replenished by those who had used them when they, too, had been down on their luck. A Salt of the Earth box, it is said, once deterred a couple who were frustrated by poverty from killing themselves and their three children; a delinquent boy attributed his return to the straight and narrow to a few coins he found in a box near Ueno. And most of that money had been deposited there by none other than Eguchi Shinichi himself — on his daily rounds.

He was not a wealthy man. Far from it. Although once nominated for the prestigious Akutagawa Prize for literature, his poetry and novels barely made enough money for him, his wife, and their four children to live on, and poverty and tragedy, it seemed, always pursued him. His two sons were adopted by another family that could promise them a better life, and his younger daughter, Yukari, gassed herself to death when she was only 15. Ten months after that, Shinichi's wife died of cancer of the uterus. For all this, there was a time when Shinichi had only ¥67 yen to his name, but still deposited most of it — in Salt of the Earth Box No.1.That was the one he'd installed outside his three-room apartment, a 10-minute bus ride from Tsudanuma Station.

Shinichi organized his movement there for 24 years, sometimes against dreadful odds. Then, to his dismay, he discovered that people had lost interest in it, and this depressed him no end. "The spirit of selfless giving," he announced, "has been lost, probably forever." A few days later, disappointed and dejected, he hanged himself with the belt of his yukata — from a big nail in the door post above Salt of the Earth Box No. 1. He was 65.

Following his death, in 1979, the boxes began to disappear rapidly — except, that is, for three: the one at Kinsicho Station, and others at Maebara and Nishi-Chiba stations. Each is maintained by Shinichi's remaining daughter, Yuko, a 45-year-old English teacher, who now lives in her father's apartment — single and alone. "The more economically successful Japan has become," she says with sorrow in her soft voice, "the less willing people are to give of themselves without reward."

Of the 2,500 people who still claim to be Salt of the Earth members, only about 60 still contribute money. This adds up to little more than ¥200,000 annually — just enough to publish a bi-annual newsletter, which is distributed to anyone who may be interested in giving birth to the movement again. Meanwhile, thanks to his daughter's work, Eguchi Shinichi's memory lives on. It ought to. By turning his own wretched suffering into something positive for Japan, he showed a new way and left a legacy of determination and selflessness.

Isn't that what life should be all about?

Hiroshima

PLEASE DON'T EXPECT ME TO vibrate with absolute ecstasy over my trip to Hiroshima last week. Suffice it to say that the journey there was one I had always wanted to make, and for very personal reasons. And having at last been there, I feel it is a place that mankind at large should visit.

It was fast-approaching 10 p.m. when I left the *shinkansen* and descended the escalator at Hiroshima Station. And as I wandered out into the street on an unbearably hot night, Koichi Taniguchi, a public relations man who had traveled there with me to attend the opening of an exhibition called *War and Peace*, dabbed his brow and whispered, "About three kilometers from here is where the A-bomb would have struck the ground, except that it exploded in mid-air and scattered destruction over a very wide area." It did, indeed, which explains why the city is so new. Few trees have risen above 10 meters, and the buildings have yet to gather soot.

One of them, of course, is the long, low Peace Memorial Museum, which balances on stilts in one of the most beautiful parks I have seen in Japan. Another is the bright, new Terminal Hotel, where I spent the night. It was here, too, that I felt the hospitality of the local people.

What Koichi Taniguchi had told me, coupled with

the gentle way he'd said it, set me thinking deeply about the kind of things a lot of us contemplate when we are nostalgic: the folly of war, and how it mostly kills those who never even started it in the first place. I ordered a dish of mixed nuts and a cold beer and let my mind saunter back through history. At one point, I recalled the words of a young Japanese student. "Hiroshima is a very sad place to be in," he said. I felt it was, too.

Before I knew it, I had two cold beers in front of me. A young man sitting nearby at the counter with his wife had bought me a welcome drink. He then beckoned me to move closer to him, to talk. I did, of course, only to discover that language is far more than words. Neither he nor his wife could speak English, and my Japanese, as you know, extends to 16 phrases. What we could muster between us, however — mostly sign language, gestures, and smiles — was sufficient to communicate the eternal idea that however great it may be, tragedy must always give birth to goodness.

"This man wants you to go with him — to the next bar," said the barman, who had gradually become an interpreter. "He wants you to drink some more with him and his wife."

"When?" I asked.

"Now."

I declined the offer because the following day promised to be a busy one. I was to attend *War and Peace* myself, then trundle off to the Peace Memorial Museum, which had recently reopened, having been closed for 16 months for renovations.

It was a hushed crowd — a hushed crowd of Japanese and foreigners together — that shuffled between the museum's 1,000 exhibits. No wonder. The displays ranged from melted rocks and broken walls, to melted kitchenware and the tattered clothes of victims.

Also in Hiroshima, I learned a new and scientific word — "hypocenter," the hypothetical point at which the bomb would have struck the ground had it not been designed to explode 580 meters above it. Some of those clothes, which belonged to children who never survived because they were too close to that hypocenter that day — Aug. 6, 1945 — remained blood-stained and bore the scorch marks caused by the intense heat of thermal radiation. In fact, on my way back to Tokyo, I couldn't help thinking about them — the charred boots of a 12-year-old boy and the tunic of a girl of six.

I remembered, too, the man in the bar and the exhibition. Then, as we sat in an airport-bound cab, Taniguchi, who seemed always to be mopping his brow, asked me, "What do you think of Hiroshima?"

"I enjoyed it," I said, thinking that that was what he wanted to hear. But then, as the taxi drove off and we walked through the airport's big glass doors, I had an afterthought. It might have been a naive perception, even a naive thing to say, but I said it anyway — "To be absolutely honest, Koichi, I've felt very guilty being here."

"Guilty?"

"Yes, being in this place, where so many people died in such a horrible way."

I was grateful that none of the many people I had met in Hiroshima had broached the moral elements of that atomic bomb — whether or not it should have been dropped, or if the war could have been ended without it. I would have been hopelessly ill-informed to address them. What I *am* glad to report is that Hiroshima's people, like the man who bought me the beer, know the absolute meaning of forgiveness, and it is written on their faces.

The ward office

WELL, IT WASN'T THE BEST WEEKEND I've had because, once again, I was the victim of the most terrible circumstance. Saturday was brightened by the return of my Panasonic cassette player but dampened by the cost of the repairs — ¥5,685 to have a new spool installed in a machine that originally cost me ¥11,700. Saturday was also dulled by my visit to the Totsuka Ward Office. Out of the goodness of my heart I led my family there, to tell the folks we no longer belonged to Nerima — and that if they wanted us to pay ward taxes, they'd at least know where to send the bill.

I take the authorities very seriously, which is why I no longer joke with customs officials, never tease the cops, and always wear a tie when applying for a visa. So, upon seeking new ward cards in Totsuka, I contemplated trimming my beard and having my hair cut. Some of the scruffiest Westerners I have ever seen are in the streets of Greenwich Village and in Immigration Bureau waiting rooms. No wonder many of them must go to Seoul every three months. Half of Japan can't stand to look at them.

Anyway, on our way to the Totsuka Ward Office we did something we do quite often. We got lost. Not seriously lost. Just a little lost. On leaving the train, I walked ahead of my wife and daughter, anxious to get this awful deed done. I was also in a bad mood, having paid too much to have that cassette player fixed. Suddenly I found myself the bumbling *gaijin* once more. We had asked for directions and we were following them to the letter. We walked for five minutes — or was it three? — until a large building loomed at our left. I barreled inside and presented myself to a woman in a blue uniform. The disinterested way in which she told me to stand in line said that this just had to be the ward office. I obeyed her and was there for almost a minute before a receptionist asked me what I wanted.

"One of these," I said, and poked my ward card at her as though it were hot.

She took it and disappeared, returning shortly with another woman. After exchanging a few words and gestures with me, both went away and came back with a nurse. I surmised that having observed my hot face and fidgety nature, the staff was concerned about my health. But it was not to be. I was lining up with the post-maternity patients in a community hospital, which explains why there were so many young children cavorting around my ankles.

Finally realizing that I sought a ward office and not an obstetrician, the nurse ushered me into the street and pointed to another large building farther down the road, and we arrived there breathlessly only minutes before the noon closing time. No one but us was at the "non-Japanese" counter and there was no need to issue us with new cards. Our present ones, a clerk said, could be updated. Even though this rendered our new photographs and the documents we had collected totally superfluous, I said, "Terrific! I don't much like ward offices. We'll be out of here in ten minutes!"

We weren't, of course. The sun was laughing its head off outside, and we were stuck in a corridor at the ward office for almost an hour — just to have our new address inscribed on our cards. Worse, the wait gave me more time to think about the cassette player and how I should have got an estimate before having it fixed, and I became more agitated than ever. It had no effect whatsoever, even when I snapped, "How long does it take, for godsakes, to write the same address on three cards?"

I should have known better. In Japan, the simplest things take an eternity — and a lot of people — to accomplish, which is redolent of the following:

Question: How many Americans does it take to change a light bulb?

Answer: Two. One to hold the bulb, the other to turn the chair he's standing on.

The moral of all this is very simple, and it bears out something I have always believed. First, if it ain't broke, don't fix it. So, if you already have a ward card in your wallet, and it does the trick admirably, why bother having anything done to it? And two: The less you tell governments about yourself, the better it is for all concerned. Clerks won't steal an hour of your life to write your address, and you won't need to worry about them knocking on your door when you least expect it. Neither will you end up with a gaggle of mothers in a hospital, and with a nurse wanting to ram a thermometer under your arm, or trying to take your blood pressure.

I hate having my health tampered with as much as I hate ward offices. I really do.

'Human fit' jeans

I DECIDED TO PAMPER MYSELF the other day by buying a new pair of jeans. I know what you're saying. In a bored way you're saying, "Whooopee!" You are not really interested in my jeans, are you? And I can't blame you. I wouldn't normally tell you about them except that when I bought them, as I did in Seiyu in Totsuka, I exposed another intriguing little corner of the unique way the Japanese do things. This column, then, is not so much about jeans, but about trendy me, and the splendors of Japanese English.

Now I knew my jeans had to be good because they bore about eight different labels which, in effect, implied so. One said:

> *Nouveau Classic 584 VCR.*
> *It is easy to insist this blue*
> *by selected material.*

I didn't understand that one, so I moved to the next:

> *World's Finest Jeans. 584.*
> *This jean has dear unique fashion sensibility.*
> *It looks coarse and rough yet has flavor.*
> *Nice style. Guaranteed.*
> *Good feeling.*

And then:

An all — at any.

I didn't understand that, either. No matter. There was more to come. Another label said, "King's Square." Another gave the price: ¥5,900. And yet another said:

PERFECT HUMAN FIT!

A what? A perfect human fit?

This intrigued the hell out of me. I got the distinct impression that this company also made jeans for giraffes, and I asked the sales clerk if this might be so. He went away and returned with a young woman. They then dawdled off together and brought a dictionary.

"Or maybe even orangutans," I ventured. "There is nothing sweeter than seeing a trim orangutan in a nice pair of Wranglers."

My attempt at brightening an unusually dull afternoon was going over very much like a lead balloon until the young man found "giraffe" in the dictionary and convulsed in a spasm of laughter.

"No, no, no," he said eventually, waving his little hand. "No. We do not sell jeans to giraffes. They seldom come in here."

The real reason I bought those jeans was simple. It had nothing to do with the labels, of course, nor the price, nor the fact that I liked the people who served me. I may be generous-spirited, but I am not fickle. I bought those jeans because they were the only pair in Seiyu that fitted me. If the truth is known, they were probably the only pair that fitted me in all of Totsuka, or even the Kanto area. Everywhere I had gone, sales clerks had measured me, drawn in air and let it out in an apologetic shrug-hiss, and shaken their heads.

One dared tell me, "We do not sell giants' jeans."

"Whadya mean, a giant?" I said.

In America, Canada, or Britain, I am what is known as "a gent's off-the-peg medium." In places like Maine or Oregon, where men fell magnificent trees with chain saws the size of buses, I am actually quite small. Normally, I have about a 36-inch waste, though this has grown of late due to the amount of beer Big Mike and I have been sipping after work. I suppose I could be happy in pants with a 38-inch waist, or 97-cm.

But there is something else worth recalling in all of this. Both sales clerks were absolutely horrified when I asked if, when finishing the bottoms of the jeans' legs, the tailor might remove the large leather patch that had been stitched along the waistline.

"Remove it?" the young man said, as if I were asking him to perform a sacrilegious act. "Remove it? Really?"

"Yes," I said. "Really."

I didn't want to walk around Totsuka, or anywhere else, for that matter, with "Super trend" plastered above my buttocks. Nor did I want anyone to read what was underneath it:

Who likes art high quality
Do best for long wear.

I want you all to know that I am doing very nicely in my Nouveau Classic 584s, "The World's Finest

Jeans." I indeed find them "dear" and "unique," and with "flavor." I feel good in them and, despite everything — what I am saying about Japanese English labels not making any sense (I never did find out what a 584 VCR was), and being a giant in Totsuka, and entertaining the Seiyu sales staff by flexing my biceps and threatening to do handstands over by the lingerie counter — they are the best jeans I have ever owned.

Next week, I am going back for a second pair. That is, if Seiyu has a second pair that fits me.

Success: a circle

ONE BLACK NIGHT IN 1942, during a fierce air raid over London, I lay in the shelter my father had built before marching off to war, turning the tuning dial on the wireless set. Suddenly, the brittle voice of a newscaster had disappeared and the shelter was being flooded with great music! From somewhere deep behind enemy lines, a spunky little string orchestra was playing Mozart's *Eine kleine nachtmusik*. It was a radio sound so joyful and noble — yet so incongruous, pitched as it was against the bursting of shells, the wining of bombs, and the screeching of shrapnel — that it remained with me for life.

How? It fired within me a passion for music that grew with the years. When my grandmother saw how it was consuming me as a child, she gave me her old wind-up phonograph and a collection of recordings, many by the Italian tenor Caruso and the Australian soprano Melba, both singing big arias by Puccini and Verdi. Later, as I played those recordings day in and day out, I dreamed of an opera career myself.

I also wanted to be an actor, a writer, a pianist, a painter, a soccer player, a photographer, or anything else that was going. My mother laughed at the idea, but my father, who was a patient, tactful man, said, "Be a writer or a singer, son — or even a soccer player — but make sure that whatever you choose to do, you do it well."

I think of that moment, too, because I have long believed that it is no more sufficient to do one thing in life than it is to speak only one language. And I have long held that success is *not* a line rising diagonally through a person's life — a line that shows how he or she rose from office clerk to sales manager, to district manager, then to company vice-president — but a circle.

Yes, success is a circle, and man is standing in the middle of it with all the things with which he was born — his health, for instance, imagination, ability to communicate — on the circumference; not until all these faculties are developed can that person even *remotely* claim to have been successful.

So it was that I pursued as many careers as I could, with a vengeance. My first magazine articles were published when I was 14. I began acting at 15, sold my first paintings at 16, and held any number of menial jobs in between — newspaper copyboy, for example, publishing house office boy, a building contractor's estimator — all so I could afford music lessons. When I was 19, and during national service, I played soccer for the British Army. The moment I was demobilized, I appeared in several London productions as both actor and singer, including the musical *Fanny* at the Drury Lane Theatre. I then worked as a newspaper photographer and as a reporter, had more magazine articles published, then realized my dream.

At 26, I began an opera career, first by appearing in a handful of semi-professional productions throughout England, and later by singing at such illustrious places as The Royal Opera House, Covent Garden, and the

Sadler's Wells. Shortly after emigrating to Canada in 1963, and now with a music degree, I performed with the Canadian Opera and became a recording artist. I was also acting more than ever, directing plays — and writing. I had discovered that one art very definitely feeds another.

Looking back, I was a mediocre painter, an uninspired actor, a workmanlike opera tenor who could never have competed with the likes of a Pavarotti or a Domingo, an intense and committed theater director, and a commercially successful author. People who have written about me, or interviewed me on radio and television, have tried to estimate my earnings and called me everything from "a one-man cultural explosion" to someone who "was exploited and marketed by all and sundry to satisfy their own ends." Almost without exception, they have asked me what else I would like to do in life.

My reply is simple. I have had an awful lot of fun doing just what I have done, and it will not stop now.

Virtually every career I chased, however — particularly the opera and journalism — was, to some extent, like existing in a snake pit because both were fraught with animosity and petty jealousies. The thing that has kept me sane and productive (and still game to perform in a *karaoke* bar when given the chance) is that my passions for music, theatre, painting, and writing are *very* real. When you love something honestly, you can make it transcend any obstacle that may impede the way, like living through air raids. Being in Japan, meanwhile, satisfies my yearning for a certain solitude.

I was a 4-1-16-3

THE DREADFUL NEWS WAS delivered to me the other day by Masayuki Watanabe, a dapper businessman who presides over the third floor of *The Japan Times* building with a twinkle in his eye and a zealousness unmatched in our time. He picked up his phone to hear the urgent voice of a man named Ishihara, who works deep within the bowels of the Immigration Bureau at Otemachi. When officials there transferred my one-year work visa into my new passport a few months back, it transpired, they made a horrible mistake. Instead of expiring on Dec. 2, 1991, the visa was inadvertently made to last until Dec. 2, 1992. Ishihara called Watanabe to tell him I was a national security risk.

It wasn't my fault. I didn't stamp the illegal visa in my passport. And enough people had accepted it, anyway. Not until I reported to that bloody Totsuka Ward Office was the error discovered, which bears out my point: If it ain't broke, don't for God's sake fix it.

Anyway, dear Watanabe collected all pertinent documents on my behalf — proof that I have a job and am actually being paid for doing it, mostly — and, armed with this, I gave myself up.

Rather than deal with Otemachi, I elected to be processed by the Immigration Bureau in Yokohama, and when I arrived there, a serene woman named Mary Kitayama, whom I had spoken to on the telephone, was waiting to meet me. Actually, I recalled having seen Mary there on previous visits. People like me, who are constantly in and out of the country — and trouble — *live* in immigration departments.

Mary ushered me into an office beyond her counter where we both sat, neither of us finding words to speak. Then she showed me everything Immigration knew about me, almost all of it contained on the last visa application form I had completed.

"I've spoken to Mr. Ishihara," she said eventually, and brightly, "and he has told Mr. Watanabe that we can sort this matter out."

"Thank God," I said.

You'd like Mary. You really would. A plump, warm-hearted woman of about 35 with an engaging smile, she's definitely a cut above the immigration people you are likely to meet in, say, New York City or Miami. She's trusting, caring and just plain lovable. Were I single, I might even propose to her.

As I was musing on all this, she gave me another visa application form, and when I had completed it, said, "Please go to the fourth floor and buy a ¥4,000 stamp." To make matters worse, she added that she was only granting me a visa for the balance of the year — until December 1991, when, had it been properly made out, my original one would have expired anyway. I thought ¥4,000 was expensive for that.

"Only until December?" I queried, searching Mary's eyes for remorse. "Can't you give me a year from today's date?"

She, though, was searching my eyes for a glimmer of understanding of the way Japan does things, particularly when I said, "What do I want a stamp for? Let me simply give you the cash."

I bought the stamp, telling myself that from the new application form, Mary knew one helluva lot about me. She virtually had my entire life history before her. Yet all I knew about her was that her grandfather had hailed from Russia.

On returning to her office I stuck the stamp on the form, and found her trying hard to console me. Leaning toward me as if she were about to impart an enormous secret, she whispered, "You are no longer a 4-1-16-3, you know."

"Really," I said. "That's fantastic. What is that, anyway?"

"That was your first visa — a 4-1-16-3. But since then, the law has been changed. You are now a Specialist in Humanities/International Services!"

"Well, that makes the ¥4,000 worth it then, doesn't it?" I said.

That's the way we left things. I asked Mary to give my regards to Mr. Ishihara, and to tell him how sorry I was for being such a security risk, and she said, "Say hello to Mr. Watanabe for me. He sounds like a very nice man." It struck me then that some good had sprung from my illegal visa — the Kanto Area Mutual Admiration Society.

All those who scold me for criticizing Japan, meanwhile, should take heed. Waller-san, the man readers love to hate, is now a "Specialist in Humanities/International Services." Anyone wanting proof need only speak to Mary. I'll be back to see her myself soon, of course, with more of Watanabe's papers. First, though, I must save ¥4,000 because she's sure to want me to buy another of her little blue revenue stamps. If you ask me, they've got a pretty good business going down at the Yokohama Immigration Bureau.

Like father, like son

THE OTHER NIGHT, at Higashi-Totsuka Station, I saw a man harassing a policeman and, like the inevitable gapers who assemble when something unusual is taking place, I hung around to watch. Actually, I was the only one who did, because in Japanese society, as we all know so well, people tend to keep the "group" intact by denying that anything is happening. I watched, though, in case my help was needed. I didn't want the policeman to be hurt, or the man to be arrested. Not only was he a little drunk, he was also a cripple, and this gives the story a somewhat bizarre edge.

It would have been funny had it not been quite so tragic — one of those little incidents that tend to stay with you for life for the ironies that lay beneath them. It was something that demonstrated so eloquently how, in good literature, comedy and tragedy combine — and that literature reflects real life.

At one point, I thought the man might use the single crutch he had wedged under his left armpit as a weapon. So, as he pushed his way into the police box, I moved a little closer, fearing that the elderly policeman might be no match for him. In fact, just as he occupied the policeman's chair behind a gray, iron desk, I filled the doorway, posing as a foreigner who had lost his way.

The policeman squeezed past me and fled into the hot, damp night, and the man with the crutch rose almost the instant he had sat, and came toward me with an outstretched hand. "My name's Koji," he said in near-perfect English, his thin face cracking into a smile of absent teeth and inflamed gums. "What's yours?"

Our conversation was disjointed at best. "I am very drunk," Koji confessed tragically, "and the policeman doesn't understand. He doesn't understand that Japan must remember the men who were killed in the wars. It is very, very sad."

"How do you know the policeman isn't aware of that?" I asked him.

"Because," Koji went on, "I asked him."

I was sure that with the seemingly constant reminders of the costs of Japan's war with America, the policeman *did* know about the dead. Just as certain, he didn't want an argument over it, or have to arrest anyone for abusing him, not the least a drunken man of about 40 with a bent leg and a lot of alcohol on his breath.

"He seems a very nice policeman," I assured Koji.

"He isn't," came the quick reply, "otherwise he would know these things. And anyway, I told him that because I was drunk, he had to drive me home. He refused."

I invited Koji to walk away from the police box with me. He accepted, grabbing my arm tightly, and I checked, as I know you would have done, to ensure that he had enough money for his train fare home.

"I don't need money," Koji said, brightly. "I live over there."

"Over where?"

"There," he said, pointing to an apartment building with his crutch and nearly striking a passer-by, "and I want you to come and meet my father, my brother, my sister-in-law, and all the neighbors. They are going to like you because you are a foreigner and they will want to ask you some questions about what you think of Japan for surrendering at the end of the war, and things like that."

I admitted that while I did possess thoughts on the matter, I would have to wait for a day when Koji was sober to share them with him.

"So I will look for you," he said.

"Good night, Koji," I said.

"Remember my face," he said smiling broadly. "I am Japanese."

"Yes Koji, I know," I said.

"How do you know?"

"Because I do, Koji," I said.

This conversation was going nowhere at all.

"But I want to see you again."

"You will, Koji," I said. "If you hang around the station long enough, you will see me. I pass through it twice a day."

I rushed home to write down what Koji had said, and have since thought about him quite a lot. I wish I could meet both him and the cop again. I'd like to see them sit down and chat together — like father, like son, like war hero, like prisoner. I want to hear a man who is old enough to remember what went on during World War II share his memories with one who isn't.

Hey! They're my shoes!

A FEW YEARS AGO, WHILE I WAS on a journalistic assignment in New York City, a friend took me to a traditional Japanese restaurant — one of several that had suddenly become fashionable there — and I spent the entire evening thinking about whether my shoes, which the *maître d'* had stuffed into a pigeon hole near the front door, would still be there when I went home. Not that the shoes were particularly valuable. They weren't. It was just that I could not see myself returning to my hotel, near Central Park, in stocking feet. The idea that I might be barefoot in Manhattan, was perturbing, to say the least.

Now, I don't know whether you have ever been afflicted in quite the same way. If you are Japanese, you very definitely won't have been. To the Japanese, of course, this is a cultural matter that has to do with cleanliness and humility. It is also a learned habit. In 1872, for example, when Japan's first railway line was opened between Shimbashi, Tokyo, and the Port of Yokohama, those who boarded that first train happily left their shoes on the platform because they had been taught never to step under a roof with them on.

If, on the other hand, you are a Westerner, chances are you will have thought differently about this. To Westerners, the idea of having to shed shoes can sometimes be a nuisance. Besides this, if ever you left them on a railway platform in the West, chances are you might never see them again.

Anyway, I was so obsessed with my shoes in that New York City restaurant that, from our table near the doorway, I kept constant vigil on that cubbyhole. When my friend, a senior *Reader's Digest* editor, asked me why, I whispered, "I am watching my shoes, Jeremy, because I notice that someone else is watching my shoes," which was true. Thereafter, I made several excuses to go to the washroom so I could check whether my shoes were still there. In places like New York City, there are people who would steal your jockstrap, if they could get to it.

You can understand then, how I felt during my early days in Japan when I was I asked to remove my shoes before entering some restaurants and nearly always the homes of new-found friends. Initially, those same thoughts — who would steal my shoes? — cavorted recklessly through my mind. Conversely, I envisioned someone taking my shoes accidentally, then discovering that they liked them better than their own, and not bothering to return them.

Not only that, I felt somewhat denuded by not wearing shoes, and this was by no means helped when hosts gave me house slippers to wear. I invariably found these far too small. Some slippers made me feel as if I were walking on stilts. In fact, I kept falling off them.

Eventually, of course, the fears of losing my shoes subsided. I still believe, however, that anyone who is stupid enough to leave their shoes in a public place in the middle of Manhattan deserves *not* to get them back. In Japan, meanwhile, where shoes are safe but umbrellas or bicycles aren't, I now wonder: When will house slippers be made to fit people like me, and with backs to prevent me sliding out of them, or them sliding off me. I also contemplate what, when I remove my shoes, my hosts will think of me?

The other day, for example, a friend asked me to teach some English classes for him while he vacationed in England. I agreed, and everything was fine until the time came for me to meet the president of the company where the classes were to be held. He chose to see me in a tatami room. Outside, I removed my shoes to discover that the big toe on my right foot was protruding almost completely through my sock, and I spent several minutes sitting in a little waiting room wondering how I could disguise the fact.

Finally, when I was ushered into the tatami room, I curled my big toe under my foot so as to disguise the hole, and literally hobbled there. I think that both the president and his secretary thought — and still think — that I was born with a clubbed foot.

Nonetheless, removing my shoes is now no longer a chore. And what was once considered a nuisance, is now seen as something intelligent. Why, after all, spend good money on good carpets, then tread street dirt all over them, especially in a country where so many men spit?

When my wife, daughter, and I return to the West, as we did a few months back, we apply the rule there — by habit — and it is much appreciated by our hosts.

Well, most of the time. And if my feet don't smell, that is.

A little bit of love

BARELY A DAY GOES BY WITHOUT something pleasant happening to me, which means, I think, that there is quite a lot of love around, or, at least, honor and kindness. Let me review the week. On Saturday, when I took my jacket into a dry cleaner's, I asked for 10 wire clothes hangers — and got them. The woman who served me could not speak English but dashed next door to the liquor store to find her daughter, who could. Then, delighted to see a foreigner in the neighborhood, the liquor store owner presented me with a bottle of sake.

The following day, during a visit to Kamakura to browse in the boutiques and have a quiet lunch, my wife and I were accosted by two students who wanted to be our tour guides. "We are offering the service free," they said, "so we can practice our English."

On Monday, a woman who saw me leaning on my cane on a crowded Yokosuka Line train offered me her seat, which I refused, because, believe it or not, I sometimes prefer to stand. People offer me their seats at least three times a week these days, and when they do, I feel it compensates for all the times young men rush to sit before I can, nearly knocking me over in the process. Anyway, the climax of the week came on Tuesday night. The phone rang, and my daughter Nathalie answered it.

"Quick!" she said. "It's Immigration!"

Sure enough it was. In the second or two it took me to take the receiver, the inevitable thoughts raced through my mind. If you had to deal with Immigration at least once a year, you'd ask yourself those same things I was asking, especially if an official called you at night — "What have I done wrong? Are they going to throw me out of Japan now, while I'm in my pajamas, or wait until tomorrow?"

I was worrying unnecessarily. The soft voice on the other end of the line belonged to Mary Kitayama, about whom I have already told you. She was the kind woman at Immigration in Yokohama who helped me when one of her colleagues inadvertently gave me an incorrect visa — for two years instead of one! — and when a senior official ordered me to report for a replacement.

"How are you doing, Mary?" I asked her brightly, in case I needed to ease the tension.

"Fine, Mr. Waller," she said. "Do you remember me?"

"Very well," I told her.

"Really? Thank you," Mary said. "Did you have a nice weekend?"

I assured her I had, because people had done lots of kind things to, and for, me. And yes, folks, this really *was* a conversation with an immigration official at nine o'clock on a Tuesday night.

Poor Mary, it transpired, was beside herself with worry. When I returned to Immigration, on or before Dec. 2 for my next one-year visa, she had told me, she would be happy to issue it to me. "Just ask for me," she'd said, "and I'll help you right away." I think she liked me. Either that, or she felt sorry for me.

Now, though, she was agonizing over having made me a promise she could not keep. "Unfortunately I won't be in Yokohama in December," she said. "I will be going to Tokyo for training." If, however, I could present myself at her front desk on or before Oct. 30, she added, she would issue a new visa to me.

Detecting the sadness in her voice, I said, "Don't worry about it, Mary."

I don't mind admitting that I was moved — as I was on Wednesday. Following a meeting with him, a Tokyo publisher got his chauffeur to drive me back to my office. Then, on Thursday, the manager of a Yokohama bookstore telephoned to say that a poster advertising an exhibition of *ukiyoe* art, which my wife had admired, was ours as a gift. It was waiting to be picked up.

On Friday, a woman supermarket shopper in Totsuka discovered that in her society, I was functionally illiterate. Since I couldn't read the labels, she darted off and found me cocoa and baking soda. Actually, I was feeling decidedly off-color, and I think she sensed that, too.

Enter here the doctor who treated me on Saturday. By consulting his little Japanese-English dictionary, we communicated well enough for him to be able to diagnose acute bronchitis. He felt, however, it would be quicker to take me to the local drugstore for the antibiotics he was prescribing, than to direct me there.

I like people like him, and dear Mary — and all the other folks who touched my life last week. In this troubled world, a little bit of understanding and compassion goes an awful long way.

Two up!

TWO YEARS AGO THIS WEEK, I had just arrived in Japan and was trying hard to adapt to it. In those day, you'll recall, my family and I lived in two rooms in a foreigners' house in Iogi, on the Seibu-Shinjuku Line, and each of us slept on a futon. That was fine by me. Sleeping on the floor was good for my back, I remember, but bad for my general being after a bad night. Sometimes it was all I could do to lift myself up. One night, I rose from my futon to go to the toilet, staggered, knocked a vase of flowers over, and nearly fell out the window.

Also in those days, I spent my time exploring Tokyo best I could on little money because I was doing what most people do when they first arrive in Japan — a little teaching. A lot of schools wouldn't hire me, though, because I didn't speak like Sylvester Stallone or Pee-Wee Herman. They didn't go that much for British accents.

All that is blood under the bridge now. As far as I'm concerned, all those grotty little conversation schools can stew in their own juice, for the good they do.

So I decided to do the thing I've been doing for more than half my life — write, and generally make a nuisance of myself as an editor. I'd been doing this around big, daily newspapers and some of the world's largest magazines for the past 25 years. Why not at *The Japan Times Weekly*?

Anyway, exploring Tokyo was no easy matter for me back in November 1989, because I thought that if I strayed too far from a railway station, I might get lost, never to be seen again. So, for the first two months, I mostly explored areas between Shinjuku and Shibuya, occasionally venturing over to Ikebukuro. And I always carried a piece of paper written in Japanese by my landlord. It said, "Hello! My name is Adrian Waller. I am a very nice fellow who is lost. Please take me to a Yamanote Line station and make sure I head toward Takadanobaba. God bless your soul." Or words to that effect.

Now, I won't go anywhere near the Yamanote Line if I can help it. I hate it. It's the worst line in Tokyo, a sort of vicious circle, if you get my meaning. I much prefer the private lines anyway because if you fall asleep on one of their trains, people generally leave you alone. One night I fell asleep on the Yamanote Line, having gone around it twice, and woke up somewhere near Ueno with an old drunk trying to kiss me.

When exploring Tokyo today, of course, I know that if I get lost, the 20-odd Japanese phrases I have since learned will help me find my way back to where I started out, and no one will kill me, though this may sometimes be a disappointment to my wife. There was a time when she was so happy with me that she used to warm my slippers in front of the electric fire. More recently, she's been taking them out of the refrigerator.

One thing she doesn't like about me is that I explore too much — that I have a penchant for back alleys. In Hong Kong, a couple of Christmases ago, I was 10 minutes late back from shopping and she was convinced I'd been mugged.

Then there was the time I was so engrossed in Mahler's *Second Symphony*, listening to it as I was on my little cassette player on the train to Iogi, that I ended up 12 stations farther down the line. On the way back, I fell asleep, passed Iogi, and ended up where I'd originally started out—Takadanobaba. Then, at around midnight, while rushing to another platform to board the last train, my shoe fell onto the track and it couldn't be recovered until the train had departed.

The point is, of course, my wife should not have worried about my being late and having to pay a ¥4,000 cab fare. This, after all, is Japan. And in Japan, the worst thing that can happen to you is that you will be kissed by a drunk on the Yamanote Line, or fall out of your futon. I can now cope with both.

In the two years I have been in Japan, it has not changed one bit. On weekdays, salarymen still swarm like bees to and from their offices; on weekends, those same people, minus collars and ties, give Japan its carnival atmosphere, filling the trains with chatter and giggles, and taking with them resilient women and happy children who are exploring their own country and culture.

No, Japan hasn't changed — only me. It has taken me two years to relax, follow the crowds, and generally have a good time.

When mediocrity is beautiful

DURING THE PAST FEW MONTHS, I have encountered more and more Westerners who, despite having superb qualifications, are having difficulty getting top jobs in Japan. Most have been teachers. Some have been education administrators. Others are men and women with assorted skills in journalism and publishing.

"Why," they ask, "must I settle for second best here when, in the West, I was at the very top of my profession?"

The answer is both simple and disturbing. When Japanese business people hire foreigners for senior jobs, they are more inclined to overlook those with a blazing talent, or a special skill, in favor of those who are most like themselves — gentle folk who will be in harmony with everyone else around them by conforming and melting into the so-called Japanese system. Ability really *does* take second place.

None of this is new, of course. Quite naturally, even Western employers prefer people who will not be a bloody nuisance all their lives. They will, however, be quick to display a keen eye for the qualities they find refreshing: imagination, enthusiasm, or individuality. In Japan, though, these are all too often perceived as being as much of a threat as talent and ingenuity. They are a threat to office stability. "I can't hire anyone too good," the boss surmises. "It might show the rest of the staff how inadequate I am." So he doesn't.

The repercussions of all this are disturbing because they make for a general mediocrity that we see with so much regularity that we come to both expect, and accept — as the norm.

Examples? Easy.

• A man or woman who has never been anywhere near a classroom in the West is allowed to teach in Japan.

• A man or woman who has never been in business, let alone run one, or who knows nothing about students' educational needs, is hired to run a language school or college simply because he or she is mild-mannered.

• Men and women who have never been anywhere near a Western newspaper or magazine — and who would be briskly but politely turned away if ever they tried to be — become editors in Japan because they show a willingness to conform, which is why so many newspapers and magazines read as if they have been compiled by English teachers.

Here, I am reminded of a young American who confided to me that he possessed poor writing skills. When his attempts to make adequate money through teaching went sour, however, he had a business card printed that introduced him as a writer. He eventually found work with a company that prepares year-end reports for corporations.

On another occasion, a young woman who wanted to write for *The Weekly* presented me with a business car that said she was a writer, too.

"Great!" I said. "Where have you been published?"

"I haven't been — yet," she admitted.

I always thought that a writer could only ever be considered such when he or she had regularly sold work — in the same way that a man or a woman only becomes a teacher after having been hired to teach in a specific area of expertise by a professional organization. Please correct me if I am wrong.

The problem would not really matter if it were not so self-generating. If the Japanese want to pay good money to soft-natured people to do a job for which they have little or no special ability or experience, that's their problem. It's their country, after all, and their economy. The problem becomes more serious when those people who can't teach, can't edit, can't write, or can't run a business, become part of the hiring process. Naturally, now having been steeped in the Japanese way of doing things, these inadequate foreigners choose to work with those who are most like themselves — gentle folk who will not be a threat by having either better, qualifications, or even *proper* ones. In other words, they seek colleagues who will automatically melt into the system because they have no special abiliy, no experience, and no spark or fire in an aching belly.

Meanwhile, there are some good people fresh from the West out there who are waiting and hoping that a Japanese boss will take the time to assess their backgrounds and abilities. Until that happens — until Japanese employers learn to assess Western qualifications for themselves, and hire the very best people for the job — mediocrity among many of Japan's Western workers will continue to be as comfortable as a salaryman's job for life.

Being myself

ONCE, WHEN I VISITED TOKYO Foreign Language College, a group of students was absolutely convinced I was Sean Connery. Not even a teacher could persuade them otherwise. It reminded me of the Christmas Eve I entered a Montreal liquor store, only to encounter an old drunk who insisted I was Richard Burton. He kicked up so much fuss about it, in fact — "Hey, look what we got here, folks! That sunavagun that kicked old Martha around in that (bleep—bleep) movie" — that several people gathered by the cash register to take a long look at me.

On various other occasions, I have also been accused of being the Country singer Kenny Rogers, or the writer Ernest Hemingway reincarnated.

I have always seen myself differently, though. In the office one Friday, I made a very simple observation, playfully, of course — "I look quite a bit like Sir Laurence Olivier, don't I?"

Without looking up from what he was doing, my colleague, Big Mike, said, "Yes, absolutely. He's dead."

Anyway, a cluster of giggling girls at TFLC were so convinced I was Sean Connery that half a dozen of them — those who persisted in believing I was — lined up for my autograph. Not wanting to disappoint them, for there is nothing more deflating than disappointment, I signed "With all my love, Sean." I have since felt perfectly good about it because, in all honesty, I can't remember ever having made a group of people happier.

I am pleased to note, too, that while in Tokyo, I have also been accused of being Adrian Waller — not once, but on several occasions. In Canada, where I frequently appear on television and am generally known as a pain in the butt who is always trying to turn the world around, this kind of thing happens quite often. But here in Japan?

About a year ago, in Takadanobaba Station, a Westerner asked, "You *are* Mr. Waller, aren't you?" I thought he was going to kick me in the groin. But when I nodded and smiled, he said, "Thank you for telling us about bigotry on Mount Fuji," and disappeared among all the other commuters who were on the platform that day. He'd been reading my columns.

So had another so-called fan. Or so I thought. When I quizzed her about it at a party, it transpired that she had been confusing me with David Benjamin. Upon drawing her attention to whom I *really* was, it turned out that she hated me.

All this is by way of saying that according to the psychiatrists, we "behave what we think." If we truly think we are big-shots, then we act like them. If we think we are millionaires, we bandy our money about recklessly. A real problem occurs when what, or whom, we think we are, and what we *in fact* are, turn out to be two entirely different people with different aims.

The joke psychiatrists tell to illustrate this is one of my favorites: While visiting an institution for the mentally ill, Ronald Reagan spied an elderly patient fishing in his bathtub. "Hello," he said, thrusting out his hand.

"I'm the President of the United States of America."

"Oh, you'll soon get over that," the patient said. "I was Napoleon when I first came in here."

God forbid that I should ever fish from my bathtub. And I never thought I was Sean Connery or Richard Burton, anyway. Nor Kenny Rogers, come to that. I dislike country music with a passion. Hemingway, though, is an entirely different matter. "Sure you look like him," Big Mike says. "He's dead, too."

When I was working on the London *Daily Express* in the early 1960s, I wrote Hemingway's obituary, and still remember my opening paragraph: "Ernest Hemingway died yesterday as many of his characters had died before him. He was found dead in a field. A shotgun lay at his side." I guess I've always felt that Hemingway was a great writer, and truly one worth emulating, except that I don't like being anyone, or anything, other than what I am — myself.

Why must we always have to be like someone else, anyway? Why can't we make people happy by being ourselves?

Well, it doesn't quite work that way. The other day, I chanced to be in the Foreign Correspondents Club of Japan. I was sitting at a table by one of the huge windows, minding my own business, and waiting for someone to buy me a drink when an elderly man approached. "I'm told you're with *The Weekly*?" he said brightly.

I confessed I was.

"I thought you were," the man went on. "You're Mike Millard, aren't you?"

Oh, well. . . .

Unfortunately not made in Japan

AT LAST—A JAPANESE JOURNALIST with both the courage and the integrity to agree that there is something distinctly and despicably rotten about his country's print journalism, and that it deserves better. "Japanese newspapers," says Takeshi Maezawa in his *Daily Yomiuri* column, *MEDIAWATCH*, "bind themselves with taboos and rarely engage in serious investigative reporting. Most major scandals over the past 15 years, with the exception of the Recruit bribes-for-political favors scandal, were first disclosed by media other than newspapers, or by the foreign press."

We need a few more people like him in Japanese journalism. Even when newspapers were first with an important story — like the recent securities scandal — Maezawa points out, they rarely ran them before the results of investigations were leaked. Additionally, Japanese reporters customarily cultivate tight, exclusive relationships with politicians and government bureaucrats, and members of editorial committees at major Japanese newspapers sit on government advisory councils and help formulate policy. This, Maezawa contends, means that if ever their editors want to criticize the government, they can't.

Now I've never met a Japanese journalist who has wanted to criticize the government, nor anyone else, come to that. This is why experienced Western journalists consider Japanese journalism both perplexing and inadequate.

Why, exactly? And why don't those Japanese people already in journalism learn more about it and develop journalistic judgment? Beyond what Maezawa says, the reasons are, I think, two-fold. First, too many of the men who run Japan's newspapers and magazines — the executive editors, mostly, and their underlings — know very little about modern-day journalism and what it should do. They know that their publications must make money, of course. But they lack the knowledge of what should go in them, and in what form.

Japanese editors very rarely speak in terms of sharp, crisp news stories or powerful, human features. Nor of stinging editorials. I've not yet heard of such descriptions in Japan. On the contrary, one well-known Japanese editor frequently tells his staffers to make articles and headings as dull as they possibly can so as not to upset the establishment. "Keep it wooden," he says. To young people who are fresh to the business, and who know no better, this man is a dreadful role model.

In the West, of course, we learn very early how absolutely not to make writing wooden. And if we persist in making it so, we lose our jobs. The basis of all journalism, after all, is to reveal the real world accurately and faithfully. In the print media, solid, pertinent facts must be delivered in a lively writing style that will attract and inform a lot of readers. Only in Japan, it seems, where newspapers are edited by salarymen, is "wooden" writing seen as honorable.

The second reason why Japanese journalism is ineffectual is this: Proper journalism calls for an objectively critical view of the world. So, to gather those pertinent facts, a certain amount of confrontation is often required. Neither of these qualities, of course, comes naturally to the Japanese. The moment they start school, they are taught to obey, not to contest; to follow, not to lead; to be grateful for what they have, even though this may not be sufficient, and not to fight for more; to honor authority, no matter how questionable it may be, and not to cause its downfall. Children grow up impervious to their country's faults, believing that if they protect their culture and preserve a non-critical environment, they will automatically be lead forth to prosperity.

Unfortunately, such teachings do not spawn journalists, and never did. The kind of journalism that inspires, motivates, or forces governments to make a system more equitable, requires a talent for investigation. And all investigation is predicated on the very simple assumption that people — particularly politicians — do not always tell the truth.

Proper journalism, then, is no place for the superstitious or the wide-eyed. If, then, you think that racism, sexism, or chauvinism are fine, or that single-parent women should continue to be victimized, or that key money is not an unwarranted gift to a greedy landlord, or that gray-haired old salaryman with no apparent ability — like some of the editors Takeshi Maezawa and I both know — should be free to manipulate men and women who are more talented than themselves, or that nothing need ever be done to change these things, then journalism is not for you. Under these circumstances, I wouldn't bother with it. I'd find something else to do.

Let the reporters do their jobs

ONE OF THE BIGGEST PROBLEMS with Japanese journalism is that over the years, the people in it — the reporters, the writers, the publishers — have allowed government and big business to dictate to them. They have let them interfere with the way a story is to be told, or even if it is to be told at all. In late July, remember, the weekly magazine *Themis* folded after it became known that its owner had bowed to government pressure to kill a story that was supposedly critical of the Tax Agency.

No proper publisher who considered his readers would have given in so easily, of course. He would have fought for what is right — and published the story anyway. So, when the government actually told him to close down, maybe he got what he deserved. In a democracy — which journalism must help refine and protect — no publishers can afford to be told what to include in his or her magazine, or what to leave out.

This dreadful business of letting outside forces control the news explains why the source of far too much of what is printed in Japan's newspapers is, as you will have noticed, a government or industrial study or report. In the West, reporters are taught how to be wary of such documents because they might just be mere propaganda, which they often are. Here in Japan, though, attitudes to authority are so different that whatever governments or industry say, is printed without question, as if it were the *Holy Gospel.*

This has been going on for so long that industry and governments have effectively learned to tame Japanese reporters, so that press conferences are rarely what they are supposed to be — confrontational; reporters simply return to their newspapers and write exactly what has been expected of them, carefully avoiding any kind of controversy.

An American ecologist told me recently how she attended a press conference at which Japanese environmentalists were to have confronted Japan's environment minister about the state of his nation's beaches, particularly those within an hour or so from Tokyo. "But everyone just sat there nodding their heads," she said, "without even asking a single question. And all the newspaper reporters did the same."

This point, and others, are somewhat substantiated in Takeshi Maezawa's *MEDIAWATCH* column in *The Daily Yomiuri.* This unusually honest critique of Japanese journalism also reveals how Japanese journalists are "under too much pressure" to protest against what Maezawa calls "controls on information."

Never mind big business and powerful governments. Maezawa cites a case that shows how news coverage has been censored by Japanese traditions and superstitions! Last October, for instance, a *Yomiuri* reporter was apparently denied access to a celebration that marked the completion of a highway tunnel in Yamagata because the workers honestly believed that the presence of a woman would "anger the goddess of the mountain" and cause a critical accident. Despite repeated requests to cover the ceremonial speeches and take photographs of the guests, the woman was led away.

The legal system also encourages censorship, it seems. When another *Yomiuri* reporter entered the Kanazawa District Court to cover a class-action suit against a nuclear power station, she found that the chief judge had posted, on the door of the lawyers' waiting room, an injunction that prohibited news gathering in the courthouse. Exercising her news sense, the woman then tried to take a photograph of the notice. As she did so, about 10 courtroom officials obeyed the judge's orders and stood menacingly in her way.

Both this, and the case of the mountain "goddess" were eventually resolved. The Highway Public Corporation apparently convinced construction companies who built the tunnel that "goddesses" actually like women reporters, and the Kanazawa court judge apologized for his "inappropriate" action. But the damage had been done. Readers, who are the most important characters in all of this, were deprived of important facts that were undeniably in the public domain.

Questions still remain, however, about whether this kind of thing will ever happen again and, if it does, to what lengths Japan's journalists are prepared to go — to fight it. None, I suspect. But if they want to upgrade their profession to conform to Western standards, and thereby help to "internationalize" their country as they go, they must cast off some of their cultural niceties and start telling governments and big business that, for the sake of democracy, they must no longer interfere.

Letter to the folks back home

DEAR ALL: At last, I have time to write to you. As you know, after our return here in early June we had to spend at least two months re-establishing ourselves, and this took a lot of energy, not to mention money. We promised ourselves, however, that we would find an apartment without having to pay key money, and, after a lot of searching, we did.

Anyway, we are settled now and things are going fairly well for us all. This is not to say that we don't miss our friends. We do — very much. But we have to make a life for ourselves in Japan for at least another year because we found things at home rather bleak, to say the least. Not only that, I feel comfortable in Japan. I'd rather see a group society like Japan's amble along sociably than be part of a society of individuals that is dominated by horrible crime and seemingly continuous labor unrest.

In this respect, we have received very few letters from Montreal since our return because of Canada's recent mail strike. Canada's propensity for strikes, coupled with the uncertain political climate in Quebec, should also tell you something about why we decided to return here. From the standpoint of being able to escape Quebec politics, I am happy to be here; once having actually owned a house in Montreal seems so distant now. So we don't really fret for that, either. Maybe that's because we know we will always be able to afford another, better home, though whether or not this will be in Montreal — or even Canada — remains to be seen.

I confess to spending many nights here wondering what can possibly be next for us. We can't live in Japan forever because, as much as we would like to, too many things here are against us. Daily life is far from easy, particularly when you consider the climate, the amount of time we must work to make a decent living, and how cultural attitudes sometimes tend to stick in my throat.

When, for instance, a young colleague heard that we had found an apartment without key money, she was quick to observe, "That's not fair. We Japanese have to pay that!"

I replied, "That's your fault. If you don't agree with something, fight it!"

She never will, though. The Japanese don't seem to have any fight in them, and it is frankly disturbing to see this nearly every day. On top of this, we will never be able to speak the local language.

I also spend time wondering what country we would next like to live in. Ideally, we should find some semi-tropical haven where our retirement incomes will be worth a lot more than they at present are. Hong Kong is a marvelous place. So is Singapore, Thailand, even Malaysia. Whoever thought that in terms of economic power and improvement in the quality of life, the latter two or three decades of this century would belong to Asia!

Well, they do, and if ever you see Japan, you will realize how much hard work went into rekindling an industrial revolution that has set the world on its ear.

Our biggest problem, however, really has nothing to do with climate, earning a living, or customs, nor affording some of life's little luxuries. It is deeper than that. We ask ourselves how, when the time comes, we will ever be able to settle in the West again. Japan has virtually no street crime, remember, no strikes, no violent demonstrations, no threat to public safety, and almost no unemployment. The economy, though ailing a little of late, is so strong that you would never suspect how other parts of the world have been plunged into a deep recession.

On other matters, I have had another two teeth capped and have bought a VCR and a portable CD player. Hence we have been building a collection of CDs, most of which have cost us about ¥1,000 ($7.50) each — one of the few bargains available in Japan, I would say. The other day, for instance, I bought some real gems for this price: two Schubert song cycles sung by baritone Dietrich Fischer-Dieskau, some operatic arias sung by tenor Luciano Pavarotti, as well as Mozart's four great horn concertos.

How music has made my life! On blustery nights, when the wind drives the rain against our windows furiously, I lie in bed listening to Mozart or Wagner, and generally being thankful that the choice of whether or not we will stay in Japan is truly ours. Most people cannot choose where they want to live. Most people in this horrible world are struggling with the day-to-day worry of when, or if, they will eat. In this respect we are lucky, indeed.

When the time comes for us to leave Japan, it will not be easy — for any of us.